CRAFT BOOK

Reproducible Craft Pages for Preschool and Elementary Students!

See our Special HomeLink Activities!

NOAH'S PARK® CHILDREN'S CHURCH CRAFT BOOK (Red Edition)
Published by David C. Cook
4050 Lee Vance View
Colorado Springs, CO 80918 U.S.A.

David C. Cook Distribution Canada
55 Woodslee Avenue, Paris, Ontario, Canada N3L 3E5

David C. Cook U.K., Kingsway Communications
Eastbourne, East Sussex BN23 6NT, England

David C. Cook and the graphic circle C logo are registered trademarks of Cook
Communications Ministries.

Editor: Carol Pitts

Contributing Writers: Mary Brite, Judy Gillispie,
                                 Karen James, Gail Rohlfing,
                                 Scott Stewart, Nancy Sutton

Interior Design: Mike Riester

Cover Design: Todd Mock

Illustrations: Aline Heiser, Chris Sharp

All Scripture quotations, unless otherwise noted, are taken from the HOLY BIBLE, NEW
INTERNATIONAL VERSION®. Copyright © 1973, 1978, 1984 by International Bible Society.
Used by permission of Zondervan. All rights reserved.

ISBN 978-0-7814-4492-7

First Printing 2007
Printed in the United States

3 4 5 6 7 8 9 10 11 12

091908

TABLE OF CONTENTS

Unit 5 *Choosing and Losing*

Unit 6 *Royalty and Loyalty*

Unit 7 *Wise to Advise*

Unit 8 *A Time For Decision*

Unit 9 *A Time for Courage*

Unit 10 *The Person Christ Needs*

Unit 11 *Jesus the Savior*

Unit 12 *Jesus the Sacrifice*

INTRODUCTION

The crafts included in this book coordinate with each lesson in the Noah's Park *Leader's Guide*. Each craft activity is designed to help reinforce the Bible story the children have heard and participated in during the lesson. The craft is also designed to help the children and their parents extend the learning even further by linking it to activities they can do at home during the following week.

If a craft is to be cut out and put together, be sure to include the HomeLink by gluing it to the back of the craft, enclosing it in a resealable plastic bag, or attaching it in some other way to be sent home.

You will notice the designation for the activities. **RCE** refers to the Elementary Craft in the Red Edition of Noah's Park Children's Church. **RCP** refers to the Preschool Craft in the Red Edition of the Noah's Park Children's Church. The number following that designation identifies the lesson number.

Each craft activity has a list of supplies listed which you will want to gather prior to your session. You may want to make one of the crafts in advance so that you can show the children what they will make. This will also assist the Park Patrol members as they help the children.

There are some basic supplies that you should keep on hand. These are listed below. Other supplies are more specialized and should be gathered as needed.

Pencils with erasers

Markers

Drawing paper

Construction paper (variety of colors, both 9" x 12" and 12" x 18")

Tape

Glue, paste, or glue sticks

Scissors

Craft sticks

Paper fasteners, paper clips

Stapler and staples

Yarn, glitter, confetti

Resealable plastic bags (sandwich size)

RCE1: Heavenly Mobile

Supplies: Cardboard, scissors, string or yarn, construction paper, pencils, hole punch, metal clothes hangers, clear tape, crayons, copies of HomeLink

Preparation: Cut sample stars, earths, suns, and crescent moons from cardboard. You may use the patterns on this page. Cut out assorted lengths of string or yarn.

Directions: Hand out construction paper and pencils to the children. Set out the cardboard stars, earths, suns, and crescent moons for the children to trace on their papers. Have each child trace and cut out at least one of each shape. Encourage the children to take turns and share the patterns.

Punch a hole in each shape near an edge and tie a length of string, varying the lengths for each child's shapes. Tie the other ends of string to a hanger. You may let the children try to punch their own holes and tie their own strings, with the Park Patrol nearby to help as needed.

Next, show the children how to lay their hanger on a piece of construction paper and use a pencil to trace around the triangle of the hanger. Children should cut out this hanger-shaped paper and put their names in one corner. On a board or poster print, "We can trust God's plan in creation" and today's Bible memory verse. Give out crayons or markers, and have the children copy the verse on one side of their triangle and the title on the other side. Then, tape it to the hanger wire to fill the triangular space.

Give each child a copy of the HomeLink to set with their Heavenly Mobile to take home.

HomeLink: Genesis 1:1-31; Psalm 111:2, 7

God made the universe—heaven and earth. He made our solar system with its logical plan. He created light and darkness, and He planned to use the sun, moon, and stars to give us much-needed light. They all fit into His plan for creation. As a family this week, praise God for His plan in creation!

RCP1: Creation Quilt—Square 1

This craft will be completed over four weeks. Each week send home a quilt square with the HomeLink. The HomeLink will give directions for putting the quilt squares together.

Supplies: Copy of Creation Quilt—Square 1 and HomeLink for each child, black felt squares, white felt squares, scissors, adhesive felt or felt remnants and craft glue (to help the figures stick to the felt), crayons, scissors, resealable plastic bags

Preparation: Make copies of the figures. Each child will need a black felt square and half of a white felt square.

Directions: Let the children color the figures of the sun, moon, and stars. After the figures have been cut out, help each child attach a small piece of felt to the back of each figure.

Show the children how to put the white felt on the black felt to make the picture half day and half night. Then show the children where to put the sun, moon, and stars. Have each child put the day piece of felt and the figures in a resealable bag. Then help glue the HomeLink to the back of the black felt. Be sure to label the bags with the children's names.

RCE2: Beautiful Plant Pot

Supplies: Wood craft sticks, disposable cups, colored markers, permanent marker, potting soil, marigold or other easy-to-grow seeds, glue, copies of HomeLink

Give each child a craft stick and a disposable cup. Ask the children to write "Useful and Beautiful" on their craft sticks. You will need to print it on the board or a newsprint pad for them to copy. The children may need to write on both sides to make it fit. They may use a permanent marker to write their names on a disposable cup. Give each child a copy of the HomeLink to glue on the cup.

Show the children how to fill and lightly pack their cup with potting soil to about one inch from the top. Following the planting instructions on the seed packets you bought, let the children dig shallow holes in the potting soil. Give each child several seeds to plant. The children may use their craft sticks to push dirt over the seeds. Have the children push their craft sticks into the soil in a place away from the seeds and with the writing still visible.

Talk with the children about where to put their seed pots and how much to water them after they get home so the seeds sprout.

> **HomeLink:** Genesis 1:6-13, 28-29
>
> God created a useful and beautiful world. And you are growing something that God made. Remember to take care of the seeds you planted in your pot.
>
> When your family gathers during the week, ask what useful and beautiful parts of creation each one has appreciated during the day. Go for a walk together and point out the beauty of God's creation.

RCP2: Creation Quilt—Square 2

This is the second week of a four-week craft. Each week send home a quilt square with the HomeLink, which gives directions for putting the quilt squares together.

Supplies: Copy of Creation Quilt—Square 2 and HomeLink for each child, light blue felt squares, scissors, adhesive felt or felt remnants and craft glue (to help the figures stick to the felt), crayons, scissors, resealable plastic bags

Preparation: Make copies of the figures. Each child will need a light blue felt square to serve as the sky background.

Directions: Let the children color the figures of the water, cloud, land, flower, and tree. After the figures have been cut out, help each child attach a small piece of felt to the back of each figure.

Show the children where to put the water, land, cloud, flower, and tree figures on a piece of light blue felt. After helping to glue the HomeLink to the back of the square, have each child put the figures in a resealable bag to carry them home. Be sure to label the bags with the children's names.

HomeLink: Genesis 1:6-13, 28-29

Today's square of the Creation Quilt helps your child tell the Bible story that God made water, land, and plants. Sew or use packing tape to attach last week's quilt square on the left side of the new square. Let your child use this week's quilt square to tell the Bible story throughout the week.

God made the day and night. He made the sun, moon, and stars. God had a plan to make even more! God made the water with the sky above. God gathered all the water together and made the land. God made plants to grow on the land. A flower is a plant that smells pretty. An apple tree is a plant that gives us food. What are some other plants? God looked at all He had made. It was very good.

RCE3: Animal Bag Puppets

Supplies: Brown and white paper lunch bags, colored markers, yarn, chenille wires, construction paper, cotton balls, pom-poms, tape, glue, scissors, copies of HomeLink

Show the children how to use a paper lunch bag for a hand puppet. Let each child choose a white or brown paper bag to make their own puppet. Set out the various craft supplies, and let the children choose which animal they wish to make. Here are some suggestions:

Lion: Color eyes and nose on the bottom of a brown bag. Draw the open mouth on the side fold. Glue yellow yarn all around. Let him roar!

Rabbit: Draw eyes and nose on the bottom of a white bag. Poke chenille wires through the bottom on the left side of the nose and out on the right side. Cut two long, slender ovals for ears and four short, slender ovals for legs. Tape the ears and legs to the bag. Glue a cotton ball tail on back. Make a little paper carrot to tape to his front paw. Let him nibble!

Tape a copy of the HomeLink on the back of each puppet.

RCP3: Creation Quilt—Square 3

This is the third week of the Creation Quilt craft. It will be finished next week. Each week send home a quilt square with the HomeLink, which gives directions for putting the quilt squares together.

Supplies: Copy of Creation Quilt—Square 3 and HomeLink for each child, yellow felt squares, scissors, adhesive felt or felt remnants and craft glue (to help the figures stick to the felt), crayons, scissors, resealable plastic bags

Preparation: Make copies of the quilt square figures. Each child will need a yellow felt square.

Directions: Let the children color the figures of the different animals. It doesn't matter if the animals are colored in a variety of colors. As the children color, talk about the names of the different animals.

After the figures have been cut out, help each child attach a small piece of felt to the back of each figure. Let the children put the animals on the square as you name them. After assisting in gluing the HomeLink to the back of the square, have each child put the figures in a resealable bag to carry them home. Be sure to label the bags with the children's names.

HomeLink: Genesis 1:20-25

Today's Bible story continued to reveal God's plan for creation—God made animals. Sew or use packing tape to attach this week's quilt square below the left-hand square of the quilt. As you name an animal in retelling the story, encourage your child to put the animal figure on the square.

God had a plan to make the world. He made the day and night. He made the sun, moon, and stars. God made the sky, water, land, and plants. Then God made animals. He made fish to swim in the water and birds to fly in the sky. God made farm animals like the cow. He made crawling animals like ants. And God made wild animals like elephants. What are other animals God made? God looked at all He had made. It was very good.

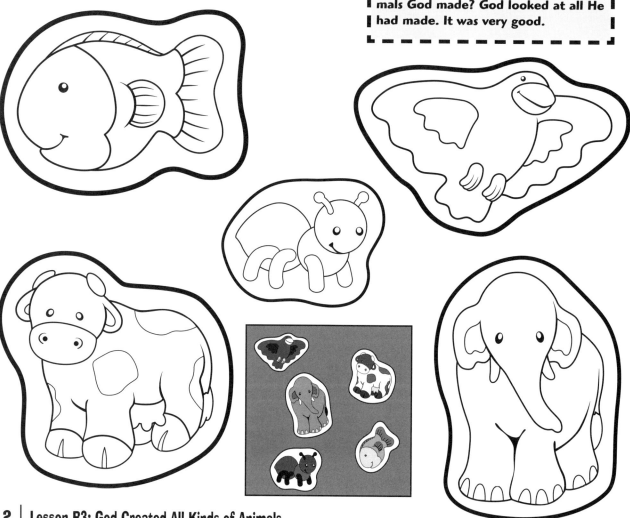

RCE4: God Made Me Like Him!

Supplies: Copies of the frame below

Directions: Give each child a copy of the picture on card stock. Read it together, and allow time for children to draw pictures showing how they are like God. You might let children tape a length of yarn or string to the back so they can hang up their pictures.

HomeLink: Genesis 1:26–28; 2:7–8, 18–22, 25; 3:8; Psalm 8

God created people to be like Him. We build relationships. We enjoy our home and work and hobbies. We are creative. We take care of the earth, plants, and animals. We enjoy friendship with God.

God Made Me Like Him!

Having fun with friends

Taking care of pets

Making things

Caring for people and creation

RCP4: Creation Quilt—Square 4

This week completes the Creation Quilt. Send home the quilt square with the HomeLink. The HomeLink will give directions for putting the quilt squares together.

Supplies: Copy of Creation Quilt—Square 4 and HomeLink for each child, green felt squares, scissors, adhesive felt or felt remnants and craft glue (to help the figures stick to the felt), crayons, scissors, resealable plastic bags

Preparation: Make copies of the figures. Each child will need a green felt square.

Directions: Let the children color the figures of Adam and Eve. As the children color, talk about God making Adam, Eve, and all people.

After the figures have been cut out, help each child attach a small piece of felt to the back of each figure. Let the children put the figures on the square as you name them. Help glue the HomeLinks to the back of the squares. Then have each child put the figures in a resealable bag to carry them home. Be sure to label the bags with the children's names.

HomeLink: Genesis 1:26-28; 2:7-8, 18-22, 25; 3:8; Psalm 8

Today's Bible story showed God's most special part of creation—people! Sew or use packing tape to attach this week's quilt square as the bottom right-hand square of the quilt. Encourage your child to put all the figures on the quilt as you tell the story. Or have your child tell you what God made as you put a figure on a square.

God had a plan to make the world. He made the day and night. He made the sun, moon, and stars. God made the sky, water, land, and plants. Then God made animals like the fish, birds, cows, ants, and the great big elephant. But God still had something special to make—people! God made a man named Adam. God made a woman named Eve. God looked at all He had made. It was very good.

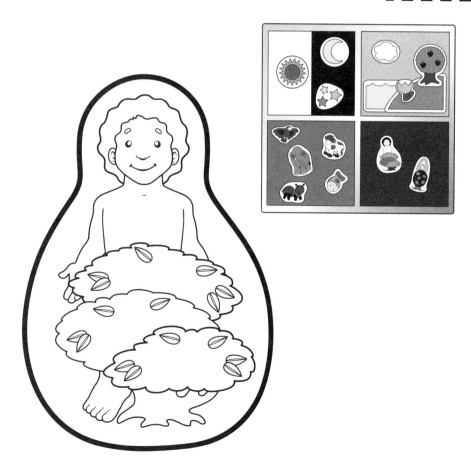
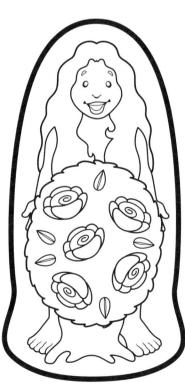

RCE5: Road Signs

Supplies: Red, yellow, and white poster board; markers; scissors; tape; copies of HomeLink; (optional) tongue depressors

Preparation: On red poster board draw large octagons, on white poster board draw rectangles, and on yellow poster board draw diamond shapes to resemble street signs. These symbols should be about 6"–8" across. (You may enlarge the patterns on this page.) Cut out the symbols.

Hold up the blank street symbols and talk with the children about street signs they recognize in these shapes: stop sign, speed limit sign, and road hazard sign. Then talk about how the children might use these signs to make reminders of today's Bible lesson. Talk about what their signs could say to remind them to make good rules for themselves so they won't sin. You might give the examples of a red octagon with "STOP and THINK," a yellow diamond with "Big Choice Ahead," or a white rectangle with "Slow for Big Decisions."

Let each child choose a shape or two. Give out markers and let the children make signs with their own slogans or sayings. Help with spelling and wording as needed. Encourage the children as they work to think about where they might hang their signs at home as a reminder to obey God's rules and not sin.

Let children tape a HomeLink on the backs of their signs and write their names. As an option, you might let the children tape a tongue depressor to the back of each sign to give it a handle.

HomeLink: Genesis 2:15-17; 3:1-24

Adam and Eve disobeyed God and there were consequences. We learned that sin is wrong and has consequences. It's good to make reminders for ourselves to stop and think when we have a choice to make. When we make good choices, we obey God. But when we choose sin, there will be bad results.

Talk to your parents about where you can put your signs so your whole family can be reminded to follow God away from sin and its consequences.

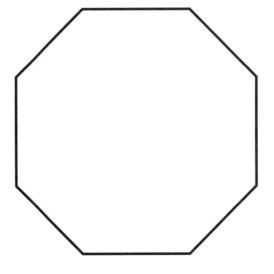

RCP5: Apple Printing

Supplies: Copies of the HomeLink, white construction paper, apples, foam meat trays (washed and clean), paper towels, washable red tempera paint, washable glue sticks, paint shirts, old newspapers

Preparation: Draw a large heart on a piece of paper for each child. Around each heart print "I sin. Sin keeps me away from God. But God still loves me." Fold several paper towels to fit in each meat tray. Pour a small amount of tempera paint on the towels and let it soak in to create a "stamp pad." Cut the apples in half to use as stamps. You can cut them in both directions for different patterns.

Directions: Give each child a piece of paper and a HomeLink. Have the children glue their HomeLinks on the backs of their papers and write their names. After putting on paint shirts let the children dip the apples in the meat trap to ink it and a then stamp on the hearts to fill them. As they are stamping, talk about the Bible story.

HomeLink: Genesis 2:15-17; 3:1-24

As you look at your child's Apple Print, go over the Bible story together. Talk about how God loves us even when we sin.

God made two people named Adam and Eve. He put them in a garden to take care of things. One day the tricky snake came to Eve. The snake talked Eve into disobeying God. Eve and Adam both ate something God had told them not to. Adam and Eve both sinned. God punished Adam and Eve. But God still loved them.

RCE6: Promise Reminder

> **HomeLink:** Genesis 6:9, 12-14; 7:24; 8:1, 18, 21-22; 9:1, 12-17
>
> God is able to save us! The ark reminds us of God's promise to save Noah from the flood. The rainbow reminds us of God's promise to never flood the earth again. The cross reminds us of God's promise to save all who receive Jesus as Savior. Hang this craft where it can remind you that God is able to save us.

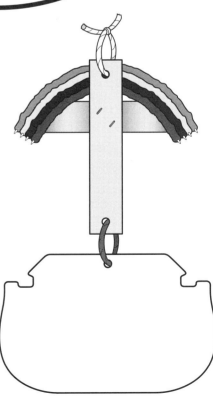

Supplies: Brown construction paper, chenille wires in four rainbow colors, stapler, clear tape, hole punch, yarn, copies of HomeLink

Preparation: Cut brown construction paper into 8 1/2" x 3" strips, two for each child. Make copies of the "God is able to save us" ark on brown paper (or any color paper you think the children would like).

Give each child two construction paper strips and show the children how to fold them in half lengthwise. Help the children staple or tape their two strips together to make a cross. (The crossbars will be too long at this point but will shortly be covered on the ends by the rainbow.) Let the children punch a hole at the top and bottom of their crosses.

Give each child a chenille wire in each of the four colors. Explain that they should bend the wires to make a rainbow. Help the children place a piece of tape across the top of the rainbow (wrapped front and back) to hold the wires together. Then help the children tape or staple the top curve of their rainbows *behind* the top of their crosses, beneath the hole. They should place the ends of the rainbows *in front of* the crosspiece of the cross.

Give out the arks and read together what it says. Let the children cut out the arks and punch a hole in the top of each. Help the children tie a piece of yarn through the ark hole and the bottom of the cross so the ark hangs beneath it. Help the children tie another piece of yarn through the hold at the top of the cross to serve as a hanger. Tape a copy of HomeLink to the back of each ark.

RCP6: Rainbow Stick

Supplies: Copies of the HomeLink; paper towel tubes; crepe paper streamers in red, yellow, orange, green, blue, and purple; glue sticks; packing tape; crayons

Preparation: Cut an 18-inch length of each color streamer for each child.

Directions: Give each child a paper towel tube and a HomeLink. Have the children glue their HomeLinks around the tube. Let the children stack up each color of streamer, then help tape the stack of streamers to one end of the tube. Encourage children to decorate the paper towel with crayons.

> **HomeLink:** Genesis 6:9, 12-14; 7:24; 8:1, 18, 21-22; 9:1, 12-17
>
> **Noah obeyed God. God told Noah to build a big boat. Noah, his family, and all the animals lived on the boat. God sent rain for 40 days and 40 nights to cover all the land. When all the water went away, Noah and the animals came out of the boat. Noah thanked God for keeping them safe. God put a rainbow in the sky as a promise that God is able to save us.**
>
> Let your child wave the Rainbow Stick as a way of remembering that God is able to save us.

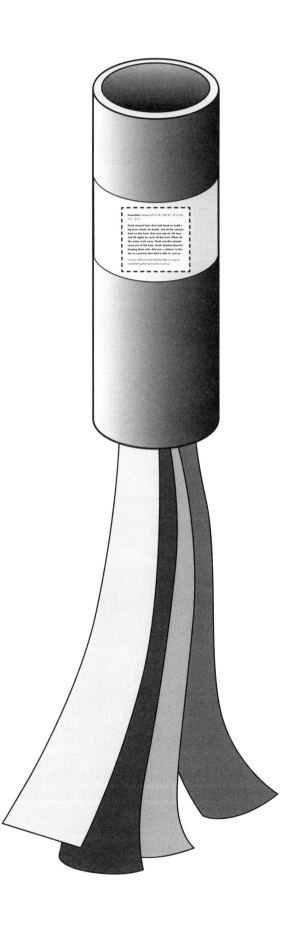

RCE7: Promise Posters

Supplies: 9" x 12" sheets of regular craft foam in one color, 9" x 12" sheets of sticky-back craft foam in a second color, assorted precut craft foam shapes, scissors, tape, craft glue, colored markers or ballpoint pens, copies of HomeLink

Preparation: One inch in from the edges, cut a rectangle from the sticky-back craft foam, forming a frame with the one-inch edge. Make one for each child. From the leftover cut-out rectangles, make Bible outlines by tracing the shape below. Cut them out, preparing one for each child.

Give each child a sheet of regular craft foam in the first color and a cut-out frame of sticky-back craft foam. Show the children how to peel the backing from the frame and attach it over top of the non-sticky foam to make a picture frame. Have the children put their names on the back of their pictures. Tape a copy of the HomeLink to the back of each picture.

Show the foam Bible shape and talk about how God's promises to us are in the Bible. Give each child a Bible shape to attach to the center of their picture frame. On the board print "God Keeps All His Promises" for children to carefully copy onto their pictures, above and below the Bible, using markers or pens.

Let the children choose from among the assorted precut foam shapes to decorate their frames, using glue to attach the shapes. Set aside to let the glue dry before sending home.

Encourage Park Patrol members to help as needed and to ask the children to name promises from God.

HomeLink: Genesis 18:1-16; 21:1-6

God keeps all His promises. He kept His promise to Abraham, even though it didn't seem possible. God keeps all His promises in the Bible.

Hang up your poster at home. Ask your parents to share ways they experience God's keeping His promises in their lives.

RCP7: Promise Pillow

Supplies: Copies of the HomeLink, two half sheets of white construction paper for each child, glue sticks, old newspapers or paper towels, star stickers, washable markers, packing tape

Preparation: Photocopy the "God keeps all His promises" rectangle on one sheet of paper for each child.

Directions: Give each child a blank sheet of paper and one with the photocopy on it. Let the children glue a HomeLink to the paper without the rectangle. Give out stars and let the children choose where to put them on their papers. Let the children further color and decorate their papers.

Help each child tape three sides of the papers together to make a pillowcase. Then they lightly stuff their cases with newspaper or paper towels. Tape the fourth side together.

HomeLink: Genesis 18:1-16; 21:1-6

Put this Promise Pillow in a special place throughout the week to remember that God keeps His promises.

Abraham was 100 years old. Hold up one finger. **Sarah, his wife, was very old too.** Hold up a second finger. **God said they would have a baby boy. Baby Isaac was born.** Pretend to rock a baby. **God keeps His promises.**

RCE8: Travel Passport

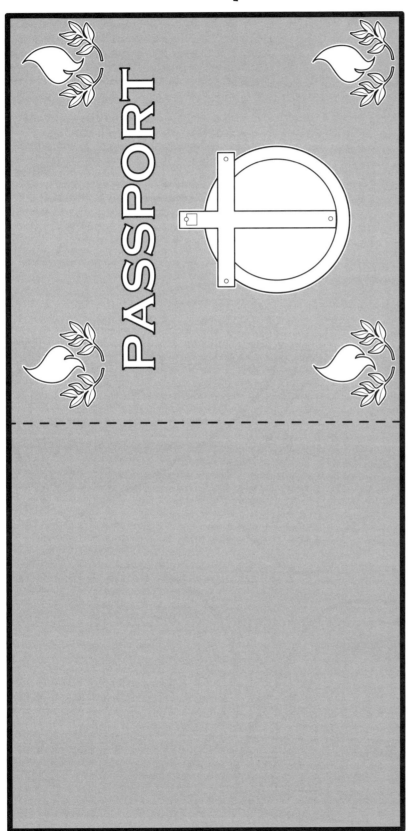

Supplies: Copies of the passport cover, white paper, stapler, pencils, colored pencils

Preparation: Copy the passport cover on stiff paper for each child. Cut white paper into thirds. Trim the edges so they will fit inside the covers.

Give each child a passport cover and two or three white pages. Show the children how to stack them together and fold in half to make a booklet. Let Park Patrol members staple each child's booklet.

On the board demonstrate how to list key information: name, address, age, and physical descriptions. The children should write this information about themselves on the inside front cover of their passport.

On the first page, children write, "God helps me when I ask" and draw self-portraits. The remaining pages are for the children's pictures and words about how God has helped them or what they might ask God for help with. Allow the children time to draw and discuss their ideas and experiences.

HomeLink: Genesis 24

We all need help at times. And God is just the person to ask for help. The Bible story about Abraham's servant is a good example.

What do you need help with? Talk it over with your parents. Then pray with them, asking God for His help. God helps us when we ask!

RCP8: Isaac and Rebekah Bible Puppets

Supplies: Copies of the puppets and HomeLink, craft sticks, crayons, scissors, transparent tape, resealable plastic bags

Preparation: Make copies of this page so that each child has a set of five puppet figures. Cut out the puppets for younger preschoolers ahead of time.

Directions: Give each child a set of five puppet figures to color. Older preschoolers will be able to cut out their own puppets. Help the children tape a craft stick to the back of each puppet to serve as a handle. Put each child's puppets in a resealable bag, along with a HomeLink, to take home.

HomeLink: Genesis 24

Encourage your child to use the puppets while telling the Bible story throughout the week.

Abraham asked his servant to go find a wife for Isaac. The servant and his camels traveled a long way. They came to a well. The servant prayed and asked God to help him. Rebekah came to the well. She gave the servant a drink of water. She gave the camels water too. This was what the servant had prayed to God for. The servant told Rebekah's family how God had helped him find Rebekah. He asked if she could be Isaac's wife. The servant and Rebekah traveled back to Abraham. Isaac and Rebekah loved each other and were married.

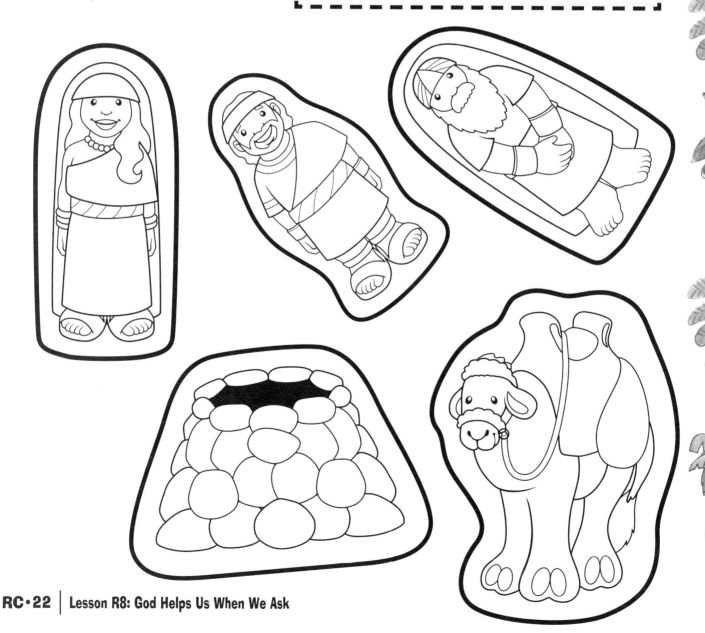

RCE9: Burning Bushes

Supplies: Toilet tissue tubes; hole punch; pencils; brown and red chenille wires; orange, yellow, and red tissue paper; scissors; glue or clear tape; copies of the HomeLink

Preparation: Punch four holes around one end of each toilet tissue tube. Cut the brown chenille wires in half. Cut the red wires in thirds.

Directions: Give each child a prepared toilet tissue tube and let the children write their names at the end without the holes (either inside or outside the tube). Also give out four to six brown chenille wires to each child. Explain that the tube is the trunk of the bush and the brown wires are the branches. Show the children how to twist the wires through the holes to attach them and then bend out the loose ends of the wires to form branches. The children may bend their wires in any direction or shape to make their own unique bush. They may attach more than one wire in some holes.

Give out red wires and show the children how to twist them around the ends of the brown wire branches, forming flames of fire.

Set out red, orange, and yellow tissue paper and let the children cut or tear short, narrow strips out of any color paper. The children lightly glue or tape these to the ends of their red chenille wires to give the appearance of flames. When the children blow on their Burning Bush, the flames flare up but the bush doesn't burn.

Give a copy of the HomeLink to each child to glue to the "trunk" of their Burning Bush.

> **HomeLink:** Exodus 3:1—4:20
>
> Moses wasn't so sure he could do much. But Moses learned that with God's help, he could do more than he thought! Here was the proof: God made a bush catch on fire but not burn up.
>
> What would you like God's help with? Pray with your parents about the hard stuff you're doing this week. Read the Bible story with them, and maybe even look for some more encouraging Bible verses. Keep up your hope, because with God's help we can do more than we think!

RCP9: Exodus Stand-up Figures—Part 1

These Exodus Stand-up Figures will be used again in the Lesson 12 Preschool Bible Story. At the end of the lesson, collect the resealable bags and store them until next week. The Exodus Stand-up Figures for Part 2 are found in Lesson 12.

Supplies: Copies of Exodus Stand-up Figures and HomeLinks, stiff paper, crayons, resealable plastic bags

Preparation: Copy the figures onto stiff paper, and cut them out. Make one set for each child.

Directions: Give each child a set of figures to color. While the children are coloring, talk about Moses' encounter with God. Show the children how to fold the tabs to make them stand. Place each child's figures and a HomeLink in a resealable plastic bag to take home and save until next week.

HomeLink: Exodus 3:1—4:20

With God's help we can do more than we think. Let your child use the stand-up figures to tell the Bible story about Moses. Save the figures to use with another story in three weeks.

One day Moses was watching his sheep. He saw a bush that was burning but didn't burn up. When Moses got close to the bush, God talked to Moses. God told Moses to take the people out of Egypt. Moses was afraid the king, named Pharaoh, wouldn't let the people go. God showed Moses that his staff could become a snake and then turn back to a stick. But Moses was afraid he couldn't speak well. God told Moses that his brother Aaron could speak for him. God helped Moses do more than he thought he could do.

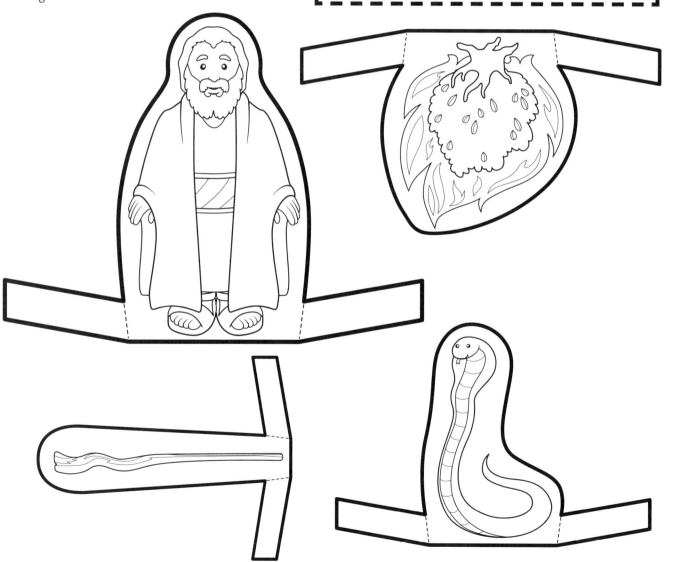

RCE10: One Way Airplanes

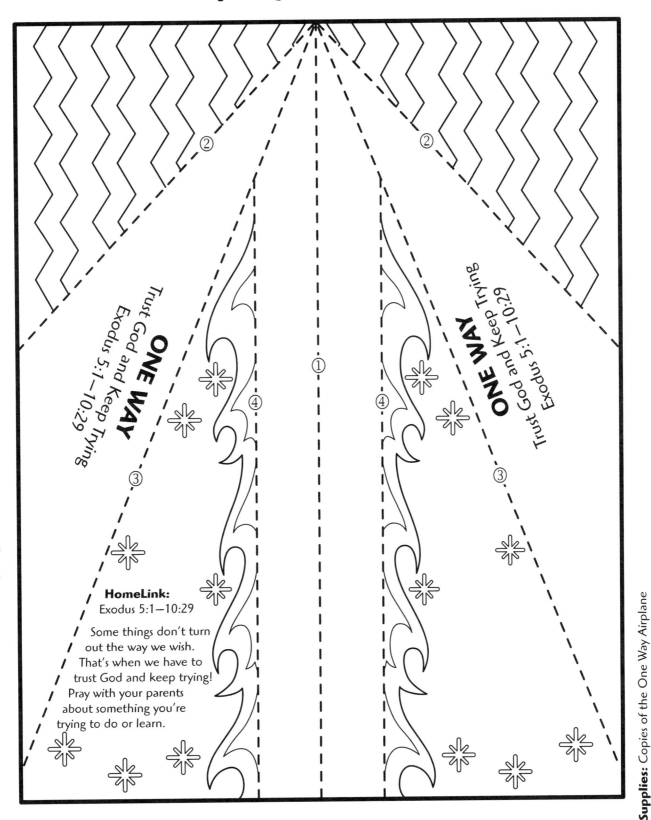

ONE WAY
Trust God and Keep Trying
Exodus 5:1—10:29

ONE WAY
Trust God and Keep Trying
Exodus 5:1—10:29

HomeLink:
Exodus 5:1—10:29

Some things don't turn out the way we wish. That's when we have to trust God and keep trying! Pray with your parents about something you're trying to do or learn.

Supplies: Copies of the One Way Airplane

Directions: Fold the plane together in half on line 1. Fold back on the next two long lines, folds 4. Fold forward on lines 3. Fold back on the short diagonal lines, folds 2. To fly it, hold it underneath where fold 1 is pinched together.

RCP10: T-Rings

Supplies: Copies of the "T" pattern and the HomeLink, craft foam, chenille stems, craft glue, scissors, large rhinestones or beads, foam meat trays (washed and clean) or disposable bowls, cotton-tipped swabs

Preparation: Copy the "T" pattern on cardstock. Use the pattern to trace and cut out a foam "T" for each child. Each child will also need a three-inch length of chenille stem. Put blobs of craft glue on foam meat trays or disposable bowls.

Directions: Each time God said to let the people go, Pharaoh said, "No!" Moses had to trust God and keep trying. We're going to make rings to help us remember to trust God. *Trust* starts with the letter "T." Our rings are the letter "T."

Let the children glue rhinestones on their foam letters using the swabs as paintbrushes to dip in the glue. While the children are gluing, measure a chenille wire on the thumb on each child. Wrap the wire around the thumb and twist two times. Remove the wire and help glue the wire to the back of the "T." As the children work, ask them occasionally what the "T" stands for.

Give a copy of the HomeLink to each child to set with their T-Ring and take home after class.

HomeLink: Exodus 5:1—10:29

In today's Bible story, your child learned that God sent plagues (or tests) to convince Pharaoh to let the Israelites leave Egypt. But each time Pharaoh said, "No." Moses had to trust God and keep trying. Your child made a T-Ring to remind him or her of the word "trust."

What happened when God said, "Let the people go."? Pharaoh said, "No!"

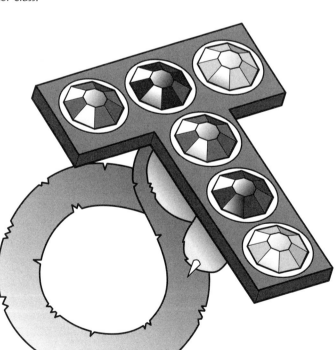

RCE11: Mosaic Cross

Supplies: White cardboard, scissors, hole punch, copies of the HomeLink, pencils, craft glue in disposable bowls, wide paintbrushes, an assortment of colorful craft items: sequins, tiny shells, colored sand, glitter, fake flower petals, dried rice or small pasta shapes, etc.

Preparation: Trace the cross onto white cardboard. Make one for each child and cut out the crosses. Punch a hole in the top of each cross.

Directions: Help the children begin by gluing a copy of the HomeLink to the back of a cross and writing their name. Then they turn the cross to the front and lightly draw random lines to make a mosaic pattern. Encourage the children not to draw their lines too close together or to draw too many or it will be hard to fill in their shapes.

Show the children how to lightly paint glue over the surface of their cross (so they can still see the pencil lines underneath). You may want to have them paint glue over one section at a time. Let the children use whatever craft items you brought to drop onto the glue inside each shape to make a Mosaic Cross.

Note: The paintbrushes used with the glue will need to be washed in warm water immediately following this craft.

HomeLink:
Exodus 11:1—12:42

The Israelites were saved from the last plague by putting lamb's blood on their doorposts. God saves all who believe in Him through the blood of Jesus, the Lamb of God. Talk over with your parents what it means that Jesus shed His blood on the cross. We can be happy that Jesus loved us enough to pay for our sins! Thank God for giving us a way to be saved.

RCP11: Passover Plate

HomeLink: Exodus 11:1—12:42

Today's Bible story centered around the Passover meal because God commanded in the Bible to remember how He saved His people. Throughout the week, use the plate to talk about what the different foods meant to God's people during the exodus. Then talk about how God gives us a way to be saved—through His Son, Jesus.

Parsley in salt water and horseradish: Life was hard and sad for the people in Egypt.

Lamb: God told the people to put lamb's blood on their doors. The angel saw the blood and passed over those houses. No one in those houses was hurt.

Matzo: Pharaoh told the people to leave Egypt. They were in such a hurry they couldn't bake their bread the usual way. They baked bread like a cracker.

Supplies: Copies of the Passover Plate foods and HomeLink, paper or plastic plates, permanent marker, crayons, glue sticks

Preparation: Make a copy of the page for each child. You may want to cut out the HomeLinks and food for younger preschoolers. Print "God gives us a way to be saved" on each plate.

Directions: Let's make a plate to help us remember how God saved Moses and the people from Pharaoh. Have the children color the different types of food and the cross. As the children color, talk about the Bible story. Let the children glue the pieces onto the front of the plate without covering up the words. They should glue a HomeLink to the back.

Parsley and Salt Water

Horseradish

Cross

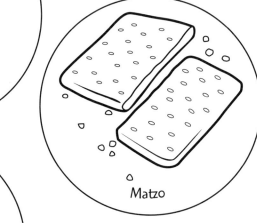

Matzo

Lamb

RCE12: Celebration Tambourines

Supplies: Paper plates, copies of circle below and HomeLink, glue, scissors, crayons or colored markers, staplers, dried beans, curling ribbon, clear tape

Directions: Give each child two paper plates, one celebration circle, and a HomeLink. Have the children cut out the circles and glue one to the *back* of each plate. As time permits, let the children further color the backs of their plates.

Show the children how to place their plates facing each other. Staple each child's plate around the edges, leaving open about a quarter of the plate. If you have extra staplers, let the Park Patrol help. Give each child a handful of dried beans to put in their opening. Finish stapling the plates.

Let the children choose ribbon streamers to tape or glue to their plates. When finished, let each child name something good God has done. After each, let the whole class clap with their tambourines to praise God.

HomeLink:
Exodus 13:17—15:21

Celebrate God!
He does such amazing things for us!
He led the Israelites through the Red Sea
to safety. What good things does God
do for you? Talk them over with your parents.
Then use your tambourine to celebrate with
songs, movements, and cheers!

God gives us reasons to celebrate!

God gives us reasons to celebrate!

RCP12: Exodus Stand-up Figures—Part 2

The Exodus Stand-up Figures—Part 1 were made in Lesson 9.

Supplies: Copies of the figures and HomeLink, scissors, crayons, resealable plastic bags, two 3" x 5" pieces of blue paper for each child.

Preparation: Copy a set of figures for each child and cut them out.

Directions: Give each child a set of figures to color. Show the children how to divide the blue papers like the Red Sea, and close them again. Send home each child's figures, two pieces of blue paper, and a HomeLink in a resealable bag.

HomeLink: Exodus 13:17—15:21

God gives us reasons to celebrate! Let your child stand the figures up on a hard surface to retell the story. (You will also need the figures of Moses and his staff that were sent home a few weeks ago.)

This is Moses. Here are the Israelites. Moses is leading them out of Egypt. They are going to a new land. Here is the Red Sea. Here come the Egyptians. What will happen to the Israelites? What did God do? He opened the Red Sea for Moses and the Israelites to cross. Then God closed the water on the Egyptians. The Israelites were safe! God gave the Israelites a reason to celebrate.

RCE13: Talent Tracker

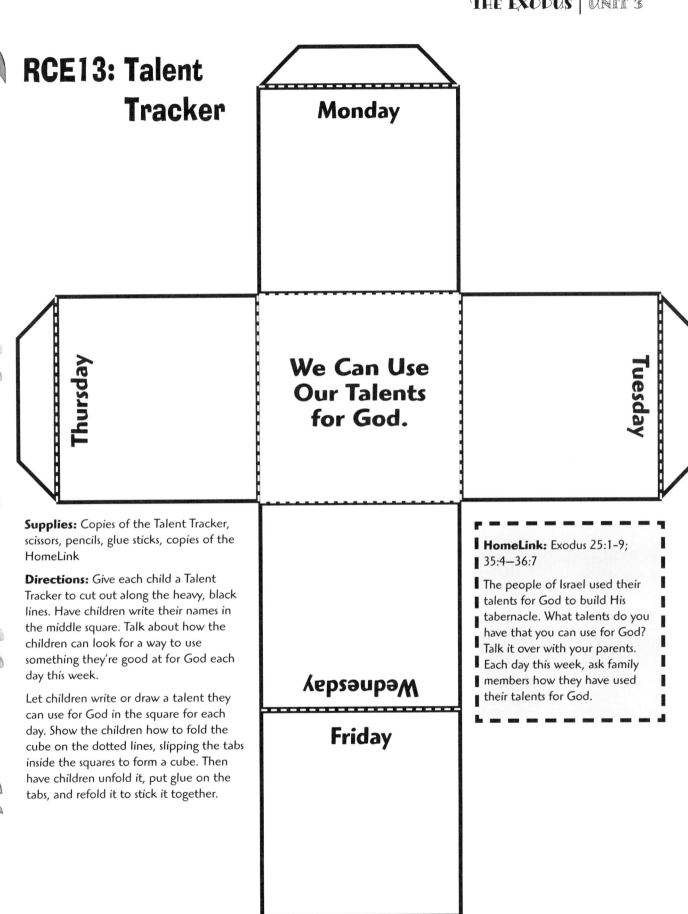

Monday

Thursday

We Can Use
Our Talents
for God.

Tuesday

Wednesday

Friday

Supplies: Copies of the Talent Tracker, scissors, pencils, glue sticks, copies of the HomeLink

Directions: Give each child a Talent Tracker to cut out along the heavy, black lines. Have children write their names in the middle square. Talk about how the children can look for a way to use something they're good at for God each day this week.

Let children write or draw a talent they can use for God in the square for each day. Show the children how to fold the cube on the dotted lines, slipping the tabs inside the squares to form a cube. Then have children unfold it, put glue on the tabs, and refold it to stick it together.

HomeLink: Exodus 25:1-9; 35:4—36:7

The people of Israel used their talents for God to build His tabernacle. What talents do you have that you can use for God? Talk it over with your parents. Each day this week, ask family members how they have used their talents for God.

RCP13: Talent Banner

I can sing

I can pray

I can give to God

Supplies: Copies of banner pieces and HomeLinks, card stock, hole punch, curling ribbon, colored pencils, glue sticks

Preparation: Make a copy of the banner pieces and the HomeLink on card stock for each child. Cut out the pieces and punch holes in the corners where marked. Cut lengths of curling ribbon. Each child will need four 6-inch pieces and one 12-inch piece of ribbon.

Directions: We can use our talents for God. We can sing. We can pray. We can give offerings. Let's make banners to help us remember that we can use our talents for God.

Have each child color the banner pieces. While they are coloring, help tie the pieces together. Use the 6-inch pieces to attach the banner together. Use the 12-inch piece as a hanger. Let the children glue their HomeLinks to the back of the banners.

HomeLink: Exodus 25:1-9; 35:4—36:7

Your child heard how the Israelites made a place of worship for God—the tabernacle. In class we called it a "worship tent." Review the story through the week. The banner gives you some discussion starters to talk about talents your child can use for God.

God told Moses and the Israelites to make a worship tent. They could worship God there. The people gave offerings of gold and silver, yarn, fabric, stones, and oil. Other people used their talents to build the worship tent. We can use our talents for God.

RCE14: Good News, Bad News Flip-over Picture

Good News: The promised land is filled with good things. God will go with us.

Supplies: Copies of Good News, Bad News Flip-over Picture and HomeLink; crayons; scissors; glue sticks; resealable plastic bags

Directions: Give each child a set of pictures to color and cut out. Show the children how to match up the pictures so that the grapes are on one side and the giants on the other. Glue them together. The children can retell the story using the words on each side of the picture. Put the picture and a HomeLink in a labeled plastic bag for taking home.

Bad News:

There are giants in the land. We are afraid to go.

HomeLink: Numbers 13:1—14:45

The people of Israel heard good news about the promised land from two men who trusted God. They heard bad news from 10 men who were afraid to trust God. We can always believe in God to make us strong to do what He wants. Tell someone the Bible story using your flip-over picture.

RCP14: Spies Stick Puppets

Supplies: Copies of the spies and HomeLink, colored pencils, glue sticks or tape, scissors, craft sticks (12 for each child), resealable plastic bags

Preparation: Make copies of the spies, one set of 12 for each child. Cut them out.

Directions: Give each child a set of 12 spies, and let the children color them. Help the children glue or tape the 12 spies to 12 craft sticks. Show the children how to use the stick puppets to retell the Bible story. Send each child's set of puppets and a HomeLink home in a resealable plastic bag.

HomeLink: Numbers 13:1—14:45

Use the following story and the stick puppets to help your child retell the Bible story.

Moses and the people of Israel had come to the land God promised them. Moses sent 1-2-3-4-5-6-7-8-9-10-11-12 men to spy on the land. They found that the land was good for farming. But the people who lived there were big and strong.

1-2-3-4-5-6-7-8-9-10 of the spies said the people were too big and strong to fight.

But 1-2 of the spies, Caleb and Joshua, said, "If God wants us to live here, He will make us strong and brave to fight the people."

But the people didn't listen to Caleb and Joshua. They listened to the other 10 spies. Because they didn't believe God would make them strong and brave, the people had to spend many, many years in the desert.

RCE15: Ram's Horn

Supplies: Brown craft paper, glue, crayons or colored markers, glitter, resealable plastic bags

Preparation: Cut brown craft paper into 12" squares, one for each child. Fold in half diagonally. Cut or round off one of the *long* corners to make a cone shape.

Directions: Give each child a horn to decorate with crayons or markers—on one side only. Let each child drizzle a bit of glue on their decoration. Sprinkle glitter on the glue and let dry.

When the horns are dry, the children can turn the horns to the blank side and apply glue to the straight edges, about an inch or two wide. Roll the paper up (like a party horn). Let dry.

Have the children bend the open end up a little to resemble a shofar or ram's horn. Explain that a shofar is similar to what Joshua and the priests blew as they walked around the walls of Jericho.

Have the children put a HomeLink and the Ram's Horn in a plastic bag. (You may use the same bags holding the "Praise God" stones from Share and Prayer.)

HomeLink: Joshua 5:13—6:26

Joshua obeyed God even when it didn't make sense. God told him to march the children of Israel around the walls of Jericho for seven days. How can marching knock down a wall? By God's power, it can. On the last day of marching, the priests blew rams' horns and the walls crashed down. We need to remember to obey God even when it doesn't make sense to us.

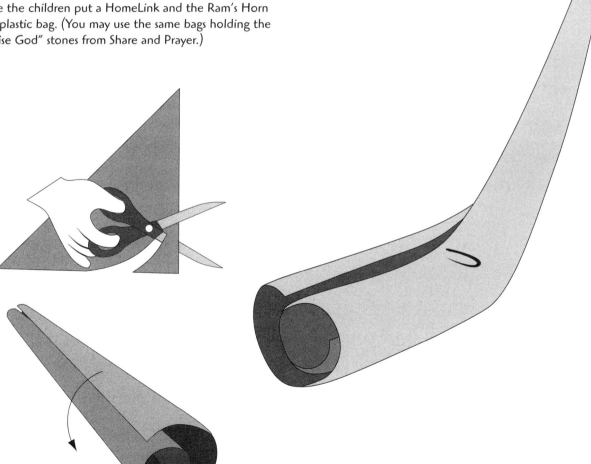

RCP15: Battle of Jericho Trumpets

Supplies: Copies of the megaphones and HomeLinks, card stock, crayons, glue sticks, tape, (optional: craft foam)

Preparation: Make a copy of the megaphone on the stiff paper for each child. Cut out the megaphones. If using the optional craft foam, trace and cut out megaphones. Prepare one for each child.

Directions: Give each child the megaphone picture to color. Help the children roll their megaphones together into a cone with the edges touching. Tape each megaphone shut. Give each child a HomeLink to take home.

HomeLink: Joshua 5:13—6:26

In today's Bible story, Joshua and the people of Israel followed God's strange instructions to capture the city of Jericho. Let your child use the trumpet to act out God's directions. Choose a piece of furniture or build a circle of blocks to serve as the city.

God told Joshua and the people of Israel to march around the city once a day for six days. Every day the trumpets blew as the people marched quietly. On the seventh day the people marched around the city six times. On the seventh time around the city, the trumpets blew and the people shouted. The walls of Jericho tumbled down!

RCE16: Disguised Message

Supplies: Copies of the Disguised Message and HomeLink; blue, red, green, purple crayons or markers

Directions: There is a message disguised on this page. Can you find out what it is? Color the picture, using the following code to find the message.

B = Blue
R = Red
G = Green
P = Purple

HomeLink: Joshua 9:1–27

We are wise when we ask God what to do. Our Bible story was about a time when Joshua forgot to ask God about a decision. Joshua and the people of Israel were tricked by some enemies. Pray with your parents about a choice you need to make.

RCP16: Joshua Hand Puppet

Supplies: Copies of the Joshua puppet pattern and HomeLink, lunch-size paper bags, scissors, crayons, glue sticks

Preparation: Make a copy of the puppet pattern and HomeLink for each child. Cut out the face and clothes.

Directions: Give each child a set of puppet pieces to color. Show the children how to glue the puppet pieces to the bag. The HomeLink should be glued to the back of the puppet. Help the children "talk" with their puppets by moving the flap of the bag with their fingers. Let their Joshua puppet tell about the time he was tricked.

HomeLink: Joshua 9:1–27

We are wise when we ask God what to do. Joshua and the people of Israel learned a lesson about asking God when there is a problem. Encourage your child to use the puppet during the week to act out the Bible story.

"I am Joshua. One day some men came to me. They said they had traveled a long way to make a promise with me. They had stale food. Their clothes and sandals were falling apart.

"The people of Israel and I didn't ask God what to do. We promised the men that we wouldn't fight them. But they had tricked us. These men were really enemies living near us. So instead of fighting off these enemies, we had to keep our promise and let them stay near us. We made them serve us in God's worship tent."

RCE17: The Promised Land News

Supplies: Copies of the Promised Land News, colored pencils or markers

Directions: Give each child a copy of the newspaper. **Today we heard the reporter from the Promised Land News interview Joshua about the strange happenings in Canaan. We are going to draw a picture to go along with the newspaper article.**

Ask the children what might be good things to draw. The children might suggest the sun standing still over the battle or a Joshua talking to the news reporter or the hailstorm God sent. **Under your picture, write a caption to tell about it.** You will have to explain to the children that a caption is a sentence that explains the picture.

The Scroll of Choice for the Chosen of God · Promised Land News · Serving Israelites Since the Exodus

---

HomeLink: Joshua 10:1-14

God can help in big or small ways. He helped Joshua in a big way. Pray with your parents about some big AND small ways God can help you.

God Helps in a Big Way!

When the five kings joined together to attack Gibeon, it didn't look good. They had many more soldiers than Joshua.

It would take a long time to fight this battle. Joshua asked God for help. "Please make the sun stand still," he asked. The sun stopped in the middle of the sky until the battle was won. The Lord was fighting for Israel.

There has never been a day like it before or since!

STRANGE HAPPENINGS SEEN IN BATTLE

RCP17: Sun-stopper Sunglasses

Supplies: Copies of the Sun-stopper Sunglasses and HomeLink, small stickers, colored pencils, clear tape, colored acetate from report covers, card stock, scissors

Preparation: Make a copy of the glasses for each child on card stock. Cut out the frames for each child. You may want to use a utility knife to cut out the lenses. For each child, cut two pieces of acetate a little bit larger than the lenses.

Directions: Let the children use stickers and colored pencils to decorate their sunglasses frames. Help the children tape the acetate onto the frames for the lenses. Then tape the sidepieces onto the frames. You may need to adjust the length of the side-pieces to keep the glasses on the children's faces.

As the children work, talk about how God made the sun stop moving so Joshua and the army of Israel could fight the five kings. **Sunglasses help us see in the sun. Our Sun-stopper Sunglasses can help us remember that God stopped the sun.** Give each child a HomeLink to take home with the sunglasses.

HomeLink: Joshua 10:1-14

What cool shades! They would be perfect to wear if the sun stopped moving for a day and a night. That's what happened in today's Bible story from Joshua 10.

The neighbors of the people of Israel asked for help in fighting five kings. God told Joshua to not be afraid. So Joshua and the army of Israel marched to help their neighbors. Joshua asked God to help. So God made the enemy army afraid. God sent a hailstorm on them. Then God stopped the sun. It shone for a day and all night while Joshua and the Israelites fought the five kings. God helped the people of Israel fight the five kings.

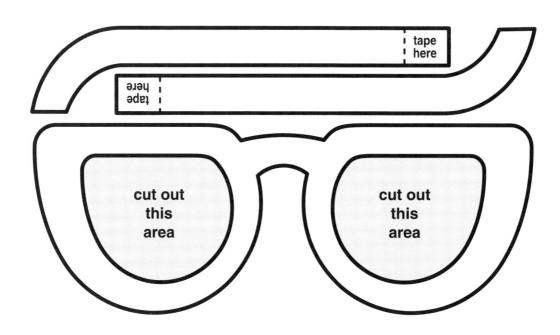

tape here

tape here

cut out this area

cut out this area

RCE18: Samuel-Listens-to-God Storyboard

Supplies: Copies of story figures and HomeLink, white construction paper (12" x 18"), crayons or markers, scissors, glue

Preparation: Cut white paper in half, lengthwise, into 6" x 18" rectangles. Fold each half into thirds. Make a sample storyboard with the words "Samuel, Samuel!" at the top of the first box. Print "Here I am, Eli. You called me" on the top of the second box. Print "Lord, I'm Your servant and I'm listening" in the third box. Also write these sentences on the board. (If your students are mostly younger, print these sentences on their storyboards ahead of time as they will write too big and take too long.)

Directions: Give each child a copy of the story figures and the folded paper. Have them write the words from the board into each box, following your example. Have them color the figures and cut them out. Then, have children glue sleeping Samuel in the first box. Glue running Samuel next to sleeping Eli in the second box, and glue praying Samuel in the third box. Have the children also glue a HomeLink on the back.

HomeLink: 1 Samuel 3:1-20

Today we learned that Samuel paid attention to God's direction in the night. Tell the story to your parents using the storyboard.

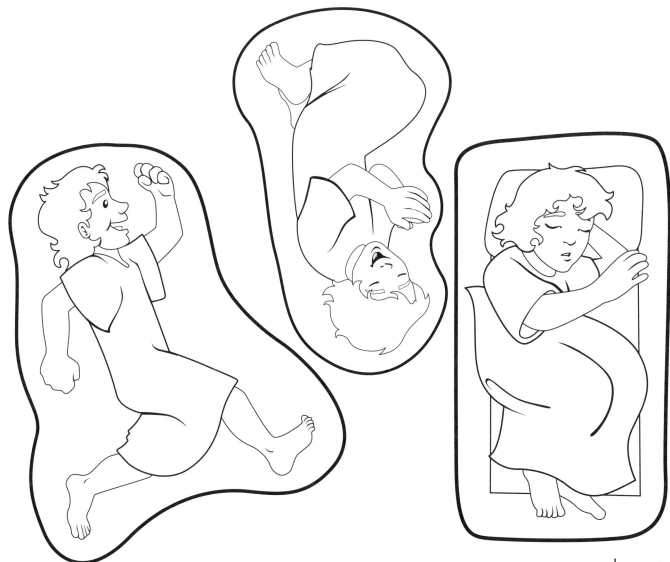

RCP18: Samuel Cutout

Supplies: Copies of Samuel and the HomeLink, card stock, fabric suitable for Bible-time clothing, crayons, glue sticks, scissors

Preparation: Make a copy of Samuel on card stock for each child. Cut out the figures. Cut fabric into 4" x 8" rectangles.

Directions: Help the children create a Samuel Cutout to use in telling the Bible story at home. Give each child a Samuel figure to color. Show the children how to lay the Samuel figure on one half of the fabric and fold it over to cover him up. Have each child glue a HomeLink to the back of his or her fabric.

HomeLink: 1 Samuel 3:1-20

Let your child use the Samuel Cutout during the week to help tell today's Bible story.

Samuel was sleeping one night. God called, "Samuel!" Samuel got out of bed and went to Eli. "Here I am. You called me," Samuel told Eli. But Eli said, "I didn't call you. Go back to bed." Repeat these sentences. **A third time God called, "Samuel!" Samuel went to Eli. This time Eli said, "It's God calling you. If He calls again say, "Lord, I'm listening." God called again. Samuel said, "Lord, I'm listening." And God told Samuel many things that were going to happen.**

RCE19: Magnetic Picture Frames

HomeLink: 1 Samuel 8—10

We learned in our story today that we need to let our choices show that we follow God.

Supplies: Fun foam, scissors, glue, colored pencils, white paper, magnet tape, copies of the picture frames, copies of the title "I choose to follow God," and HomeLink

Preparation: Use the frame pattern to cut two 3" x 4" rectangles out of fun foam. Then cut a 2" square out of *one* foam rectangle to make a frame. Cut a 1" strip of magnet tape. Also copy the frame pattern and the title box onto white paper and cut them out. Make a set of these for each child.

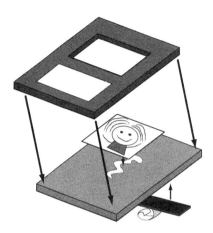

Directions: Give out colored pencils and have children draw a self-portrait in the blank square on the white paper. Let the children color the words, "I choose to follow God," and cut out their picture, the words, and HomeLink.

The children should glue their picture onto the uncut rectangle. Then the foam frame is glued over picture, matching corners and sides. The children may glue their words below the picture.

Show the children how to peel the back off the magnetic tape and put it on the back. They should also glue a HomeLink to the back.

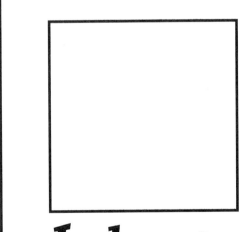

I choose to follow God

RCP19: A Crown for a King

Supplies: Copies of the crown pattern and HomeLink, heavy card stock or craft foam, 1-inch-wide elastic, craft glue in small containers, large sequins or scraps of craft foam, stapler, cotton swabs

Preparation: Make one copy of the crown to use as a pattern on either heavy cardstock or craft foam. For each child in your class, trace around the pattern and cut out the crown.

Directions: Give each child a crown to decorate with sequins and foam scraps. Show the children how to dip a cotton swab in the glue like a paintbrush and then dab the glue onto what they are attaching. Measure elastic to fit the back of each child's head. Staple the elastic to the ends of the crown. Have each child glue a HomeLink to the back of his or her crown.

HomeLink: 1 Samuel 8—10

Saul was the first king of the people of Israel. Let your child wear the crown while acting out the following story.

The people wanted a king. A man named Saul lost some donkeys. While he was looking for them, Samuel saw him. God told Samuel that He wanted Saul to be the king. Samuel made Saul the king.

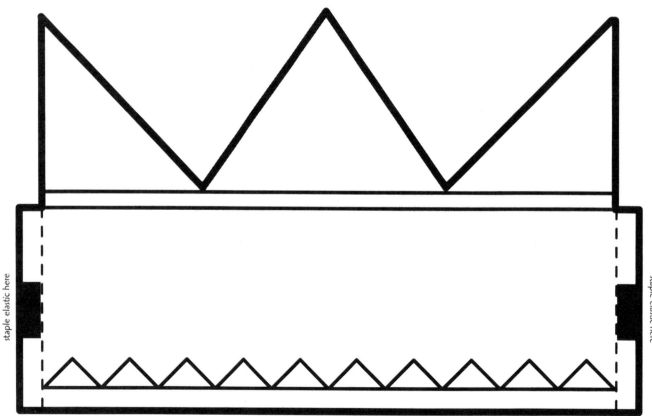

staple elastic here

staple elastic here

RCE20: David's Five Stones

Supplies: Brown or tan construction paper, yarn or twine, copies of the stones, hole punch, scissors, glue, glitter, copies of the HomeLink

Preparation: Cut construction paper into 4" x 8" rectangles. Cut yarn or twine into 24" lengths, one for each child. Make copies of the stones, five per child.

Directions: Have the children fold brown paper in half and glue the sides, leaving the top open to make a pouch. Punch a hole on each side of the top, through both sides of the pouch. Show the children how to push the yarn through the holes and tie a knot at each side. Let the children glue a HomeLink to the back.

Give each child a copy of the stones to cut out. The children may spread glue lightly over them and cover them with glitter. (You might want to set up a "glitter station" with a Park Patrol member to help and to keep glitter in one place.) When dry, they can put their stones in their pouches. Be sure their names go on their pouches.

HomeLink: 1 Samuel 17

Tell your family the story of how God gave David the courage to fight a big giant. He didn't use heavy armor and spears. What did he use instead? Remember, God's power is greater than our biggest problems!

HomeLink: 1 Samuel 17

Tell your family the story of how God gave David the courage to fight a big giant. He didn't use heavy armor and spears. What did he use instead? Remember, God's power is greater than our biggest problems!

RCP20: David and Goliath Stick Puppets

Supplies: Copies of the puppets and HomeLink, card stock, scissors, colored pencils, crafts sticks, tape, resealable plastic bags

Preparation: Make a copy of the puppets on card stock for each child, and cut them out.

Directions: Give each child a set of puppets to color. Help tape a craft stick to the bottom of each puppet. There should be enough stick at the bottom of each puppet to use as a handle. Put each child's puppets and a HomeLink in a resealable plastic bag to send home.

HomeLink: 1 Samuel 17

God's power was evident in today's Bible story where David fought Goliath. Use the stick puppets to review the story with your child.

Goliath was big and strong. He wanted to fight the army of Israel. David was a boy who took care of sheep. He said that he would fight Goliath. God helped David fight Goliath. David put a stone in his sling. The stone hit Goliath. Goliath fell down. God and David won the fight.

RCE21: Thankful Hearts

Supplies: Construction paper (9" x 12") in a variety of light or bright colors, card stock or tag board, scissors, glue, glitter glue, markers or crayons, copies of the HomeLink

Preparation: Make heart shapes about 6" to 7" high out of card stock as patterns for the children to trace around. Or cut out copies of heart shapes on construction paper.

Directions: Each child needs to make two identical hearts and cut them out. They may trace on construction paper using the card stock patterns or they may simply use any hearts you may have as copies for them.

Have the children fold their hearts in half and glue the back half to a third piece of construction paper, making the shape of one complete heart with two flaps. Glue the HomeLink off to the side on the front.

On the inside flaps, have the children draw or write the names of things they are thankful for. On the center spread, have the children write, "I am thankful." Be sure children have their names on their papers.

HomeLink: 1 Samuel 15—16; 18:5—19:18

Saul had it all—he was king, he was loved, he was rich. But he wanted more. He became jealous when David became a great warrior and the people sang songs about him. Jealousy took over Saul's heart.

A cure for jealousy is a thankful heart. Use your "Thankful Hearts" craft to pray with your family about things you are thankful for.

RCP21: Trust God Wristbands

Supplies: Copies of the wristbands and HomeLink, crayons, tape

Preparation: Make copies of the wristbands and cut them out, one per child.

Directions: Give each child a wristband to color. Help the children tape each wristband so that the tab is attached to the other end. Send home a HomeLink with the wristband at the end of class.

HomeLink: 1 Samuel 15–16; 18:5–19:18

King Saul was very jealous of David because he didn't trust God. Point out ways for your child to trust God throughout the week.

David lived with King Saul. He played his harp to make King Saul happy. David went to fight for King Saul's army. Everything that David did he did well. But King Saul wasn't happy. Each time David did something well, King Saul was sad. But God kept blessing David because David trusted God.

RCE22: Simple Friendship Wristbands

Supplies: Masking tape; for each child: 20" strands of yarn in six different colors, copy of HomeLink, resealable plastic bag, (optional: for sturdier wristbands, use lanyard plastic strands)

Preparation: For each child, gather the six colored strands of yarn together and tie a knot at the top, leaving an 8" - 9" tail. Tape the knotted end to a table. Designate the colors of yarn you have selected to stand for a letter, such as: red stands for F, pink stands for R, and so on.

Directions: Today we are each going to make a Friendship Wristband to remind us to be good friends. Each color of yarn will stand for a letter in the word FRIEND. Have the children arrange their letters to spell FRIEND, but don't spend too long on this.

Some of the children will know how to braid and can help others. The children who do not finish their wristbands can take them home to finish. Have them put wristbands and HomeLinks in plastic bags.

HomeLink: 1 Samuel 20

Jonathan was a very unselfish friend to David. He risked his life to help his friend. The colors in this friendship wristband remind us to be good friends. Share with your family how Jonathan was David's unselfish friend. Keep your wristband as a reminder, or give it to a friend.

2. When the wristband is long enough, tie a knot at the end, leaving a tail of fringe. Cut off any extra yarn. The Park Patrol can help you.

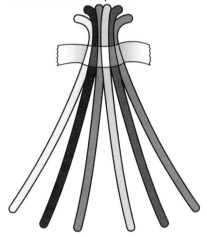

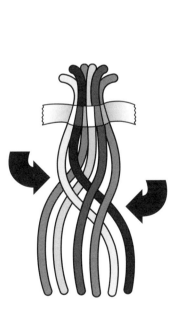

1. We are going to braid our yarn strands, two together for each part of the braid. If the children don't know how to braid, demonstrate or tell them to take the outside two strands on the left and place them over the two middle strands. Then take the two outside strands on the right and place over the two new middle strands.

3. Tie it around your wrist to remind you about friendship or give it to a friend.

RCP22: David and Jonathan Action Figures

Supplies: Copies of the figures and HomeLink, card stock, crayons, resealable plastic bags

Preparation: Copy the figures onto the card stock, one set for each child. Cut them out.

Directions: Give each child a set of figures to color. Show the children how to fold the tabs back on the figures to make them stand. Place each child's figures and a HomeLink in a resealable plastic bag to take home. Label the bags with the children's names.

HomeLink: 1 Samuel 20

David and Jonathan were best friends. Help your child use the action figures to tell the story.

David knew that the king wanted him to go away and never, ever come back. But Jonathan didn't think so. So Jonathan and David made a plan. Jonathan found out that the king really did want David to go away. Out in the field, Jonathan told David all he had discovered. Then they hugged each other, promised to take care of each other's families, and then David left.

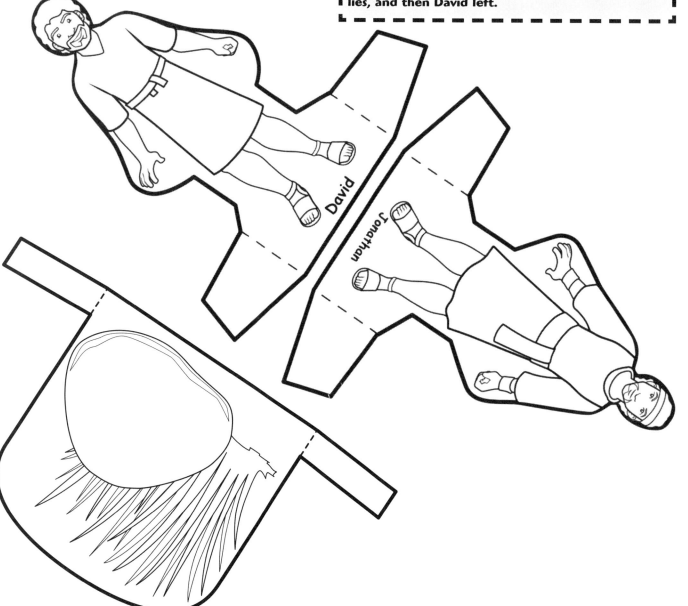

RCE23: Saul and David Stand-up Puppets

HomeLink: 1 Samuel 26

David did not get even with King Saul, even when he had a chance. Use your puppets and background scenes to tell someone at home the Bible story. Remember to say that "God's way is better than getting even."

Supplies: Copy of stand-up figures, white construction paper, small scraps of paper, crayons or markers, scissors, resealable plastic bags

Preparation: Copy this page for each child.

Directions: Have the children color the stand-up figures, cut them out, and fold back the stand-up tabs. They may keep their story pieces in a resealable plastic bag to take home.

If time allows, let children make a puppet stage for their stand-up figures. Fold a sheet of construction paper in half. On the left half of the construction paper, draw a background scene showing the army camps (tents on the hills across from each other). On the other side of the paper, children will draw the inside of Saul's tent. Glue the HomeLink to the back of this puppet stage.

Help children use the background picture and puppets to tell today's story.

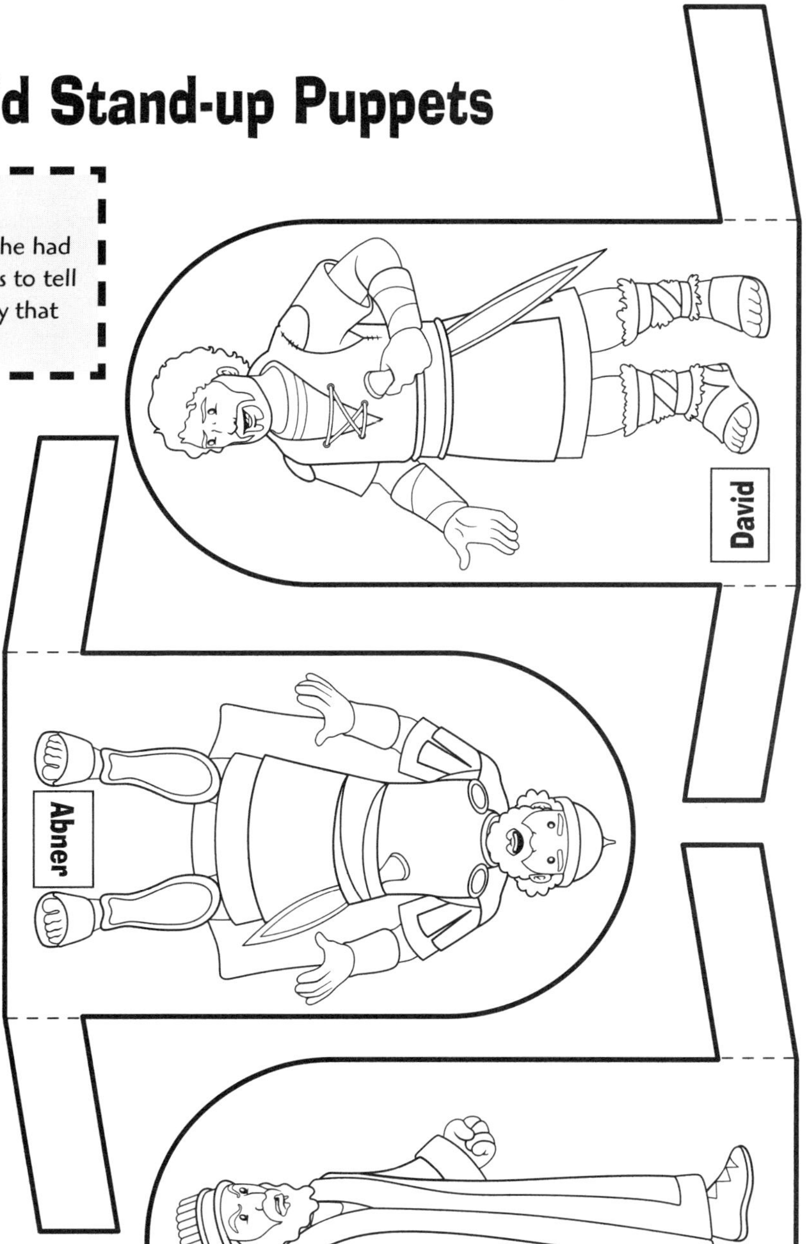

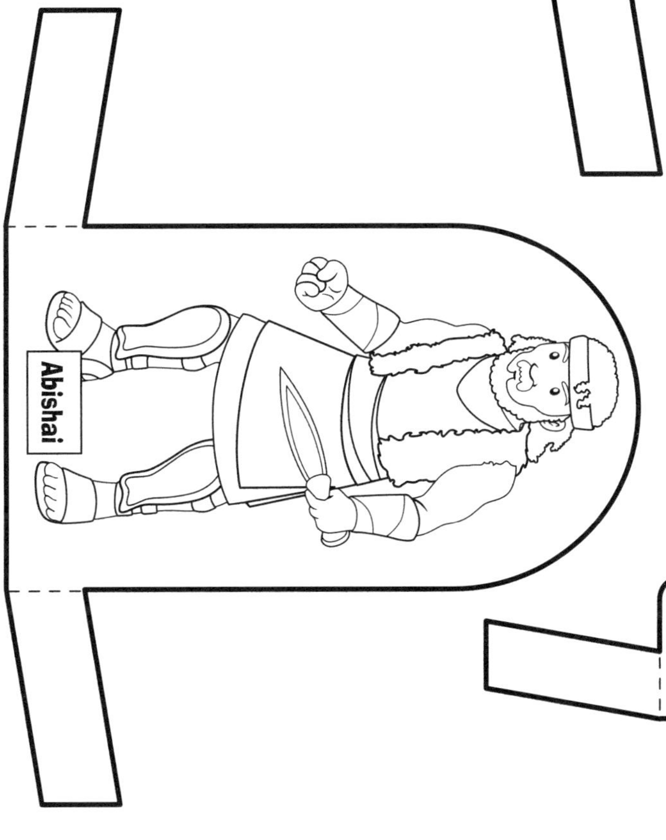

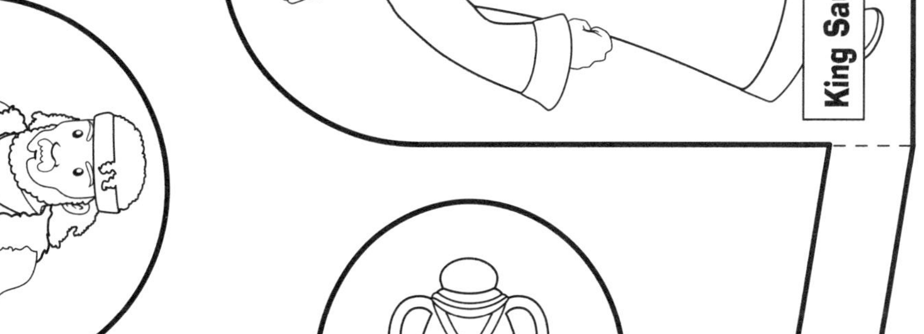

David

Abner

Abishai

King Saul

RCP23: Water Bottle

Supplies: Copies of the label below and the HomeLink, crayons, new water bottles (clear, disposable), packing tape

Preparation: Make copies of the label and cut them out.

Directions: Give each child a label to color. As the children color, talk about how God's way is best. Help each child tape a label to a water bottle. Help the children each tape a HomeLink to the opposite side of their bottle.

HomeLink: 1 Samuel 26

Let your child use this water bottle during the week. Look for ways to talk about how God's way is best. Review the Bible story together:

King Saul was chasing David. One night while King Saul was sleeping, David came and took Saul's water jug and spear. David didn't hurt King Saul because God had chosen him to be the king. King Saul asked David to forgive him for chasing him.

RCE24: Helping David Maze

Supplies: Copy of this page for each child, pencils, crayons or colored pencils

Preparation: Make a copy of this page for each child.

Directions: David is looking for the Amalekites to rescue his family. Help him through the maze to find them. Use a pencil at first. When you have found the right path, color it in with crayons or colored pencils. Then color the rest of the picture.

HomeLink: 1 Samuel 30:1-20

Share today's story with someone at home: **While David and his army were away at battle, the Amalekites captured their wives and children and all their things. David was very discouraged and his men were angry with him. David prayed to God. Then, with God's help, he and his army were able to rescue everyone. Remember, talk to God when life gets tough.**

RCP24: Prayer Journal

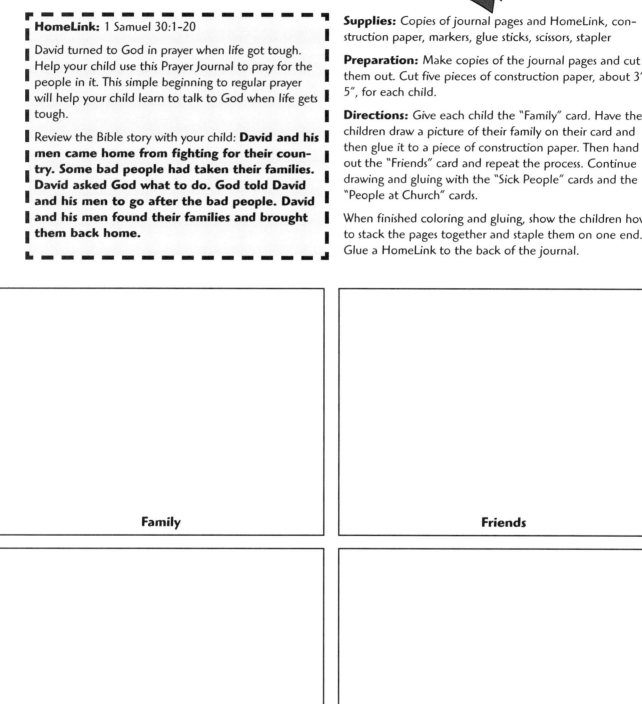

HomeLink: 1 Samuel 30:1–20

David turned to God in prayer when life got tough. Help your child use this Prayer Journal to pray for the people in it. This simple beginning to regular prayer will help your child learn to talk to God when life gets tough.

Review the Bible story with your child: **David and his men came home from fighting for their country. Some bad people had taken their families. David asked God what to do. God told David and his men to go after the bad people. David and his men found their families and brought them back home.**

Supplies: Copies of journal pages and HomeLink, construction paper, markers, glue sticks, scissors, stapler

Preparation: Make copies of the journal pages and cut them out. Cut five pieces of construction paper, about 3" x 5", for each child.

Directions: Give each child the "Family" card. Have the children draw a picture of their family on their card and then glue it to a piece of construction paper. Then hand out the "Friends" card and repeat the process. Continue drawing and gluing with the "Sick People" cards and the "People at Church" cards.

When finished coloring and gluing, show the children how to stack the pages together and staple them on one end. Glue a HomeLink to the back of the journal.

Family

Friends

Sick People

People at Church

RCE25: Celebration Kazoo

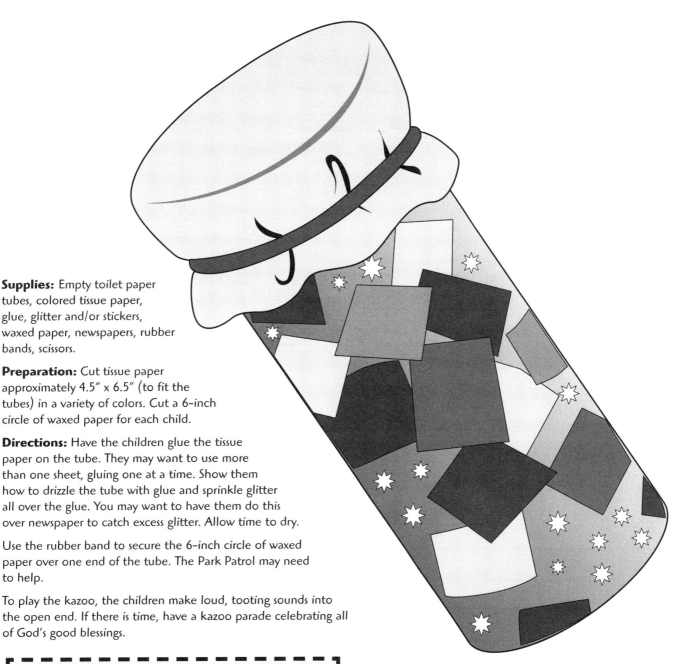

Supplies: Empty toilet paper tubes, colored tissue paper, glue, glitter and/or stickers, waxed paper, newspapers, rubber bands, scissors.

Preparation: Cut tissue paper approximately 4.5" x 6.5" (to fit the tubes) in a variety of colors. Cut a 6-inch circle of waxed paper for each child.

Directions: Have the children glue the tissue paper on the tube. They may want to use more than one sheet, gluing one at a time. Show them how to drizzle the tube with glue and sprinkle glitter all over the glue. You may want to have them do this over newspaper to catch excess glitter. Allow time to dry.

Use the rubber band to secure the 6-inch circle of waxed paper over one end of the tube. The Park Patrol may need to help.

To play the kazoo, the children make loud, tooting sounds into the open end. If there is time, have a kazoo parade celebrating all of God's good blessings.

HomeLink: 1 Samuel 31; 2 Samuel 2:1-7, 11; 5:1—6:19; Psalm 21

Today we learned about David's celebration when he became king. All the people danced, sang, and played music. Talk with your parents about good things that happen to you that you can give God credit for.

RCP25: Bible Story Magnets

Supplies: Copies of the figures and HomeLink, colored pencils or crayons, scissors, magnetic tape with adhesive backing, resealable plastic bags

Preparation: Make a copy of the Bible Story Magnet figures on card stock for each child. For younger children, cut out the figures. Cut one-inch lengths of magnetic tape, three pieces for each child.

Directions: Let each child color a set of Bible Story Magnet figures. If not already done, help the children cut them out. Give out the magnetic tape pieces. Help each child remove the adhesive backing from one piece at a time and attach it to the back of a figure to make it a magnet. Have each child put his or her set of Bible Story Magnets and a HomeLink in a resealable plastic bag.

HomeLink: 1 Samuel 31; 2 Samuel 2:1-7, 11; 5:1—6:19; Psalm 21

After Saul died, David became king. David gave God credit for the good things that happened. By retelling the story with the magnets, your child can reinforce the concept of giving God credit. The figures will stick to a refrigerator door, a baking sheet, or other metal surface:

Here is David. Have your child put up the figure of David. **God made David king over part of the country.** Have your child add the crown and robe. **Then men came to ask David to be king over the whole country.** Have your child put the crown and robe on again. **David made the whole country safe. Then he brought God's ark to his city. The ark showed that God was with them. David danced as the ark came into the city.** Have your child make David dance. **David gave all the people food for the celebration. David was happy that God did so many good things.**

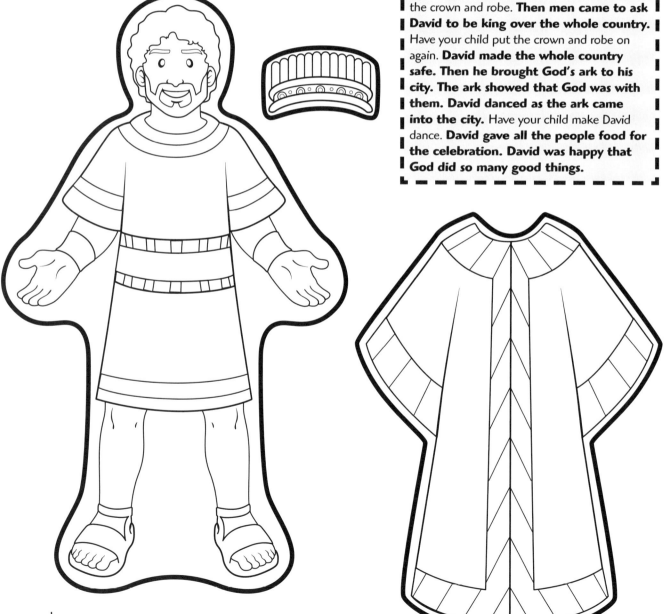

RCE26: Wisdom Doorknob Hanger

Supplies: Copies of Wisdom Reminder and HomeLink, card stock or craft foam, scissors, colored markers, glitter glue or stickers for decorating, glue or tape

Preparation: Make a copy of Wisdom Doorknob Hanger on card stock or craft foam for each child.

Directions: Give each child a doorknob hanger, and have the children write their names on the blank. Let the children color and decorate their hanger with markers, glitter glue, and stickers. Have the children glue or tape a HomeLink on the back of their doorknob hanger.

HomeLink: 1 Kings 3:5-15; 4:29-34

Solomon asked God for wisdom. You can too! Hang up this Wisdom Doorknob Hanger on your bedroom door. Each time you go through the door, let it remind you to pray and ask God for wisdom.

(name)

☆ can ask God for wisdom.

RCP26: Gift Magnet

Supplies: Copy of gift, flap, and HomeLink; crayons; glue sticks; self-adhesive magnetic tape; small bows or curling ribbon

Preparation: Make a copy of the gift, flap, and HomeLink for each child and cut them out. Cut the magnetic tape into 1.5" strips.

Directions: Let the children color the gift and flap. As they color, talk about how Solomon asked God for wisdom. Show the children how to glue the flap to the gift. Help each child peel the protective cover from the magnetic tape, then press the magnet to the back of the present. Children could add a bow or ribbon to the top of the gift. Send a HomeLink home with each child's Gift Magnet.

> **HomeLink:** 1 Kings 3:5-15; 4:29-34
>
> What a request God gave Solomon! He could have anything he wanted—yet he didn't ask for riches or power. He asked for wisdom to know the right things to do. Have your children use the magnet when trying to make good choices. Have fun letting your child act out the Bible story:
>
> **You are King Solomon. One night when you're asleep, God tells you that He will give you whatever you ask. What do you want?** (Wisdom.) **God is pleased with what you asked for. He will make you wise. He will help you make good choices.**

GLUE HERE

God,
help me know
the right things
to do.

GLUE HERE

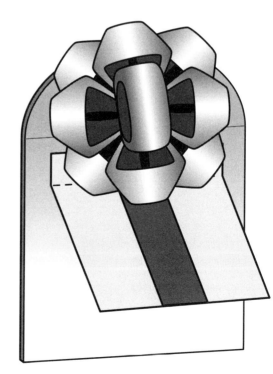

RCE27: A Week of Wise Choices

Supplies: Copies of "A Week of Wise Choices" and the HomeLink, strip of small stickers for each child, colored markers or crayons, scissors, yarn, tape

Preparation: On colorful paper, copy the chart for each child.

Directions: Talk about any decisions the kids know they will be making this coming week. Not al children will know ahead of time what situations they will face.

Give each child a "Week of Wise Choices" chart. Explain that this chart will be a reminder that God can help them know what to do, no matter what they come across. Let the kids color and cut out the chart.

Tape yarn on the charts so the children will be able to hang it up in their bedroom or another appropriate place. Explain that each time during the week they ask God for wisdom, they can put on a sticker. Tape the sticker strip on the chart. Also have the children tape a HomeLink to the back.

HomeLink: 1 Kings 3:16-28

God's wisdom helped Solomon know what to do. This week you can ask God for wisdom to know what to do. Each time you ask God for help in knowing wht to do, put a sticker on the chart. At the end of the week you can see how wise you were to seek God!

A Week of Wise Choices

Sunday	Monday	Tuesday	Wednesday	Thursday	Friday	Saturday

God's wisdom helps us know what to do.

RCP27: Wisdom Scepter

Supplies: Copies of crown topper and HomeLink, chopsticks (one per child), colored pencils, glue sticks

Preparation: Make a copy of the crown topper for each child, and cut them out.

Directions: Give each child a crown topper. Let them color the toppers. As they color, talk about how a king uses a scepter to show that he has made a decision. Show the children how to spread glue on the inside of the topper, lay a chopstick on the middle of one side, and fold the other half of the topper on top. Send each child's topper home with a HomeLink.

HomeLink: 1 Kings 3:16–28

God gave King Solomon the gift of wisdom. He knew that God would help him know the right things to do. Let your child use the scepter during the week to make choices. The following story can help review today's Bible story.

Two women both said they were the mother of a baby boy. King Solomon asked a question. The baby's mother answered the question by showing love for her baby. King Solomon said that she should keep her baby boy because the other woman didn't care what happened to him.

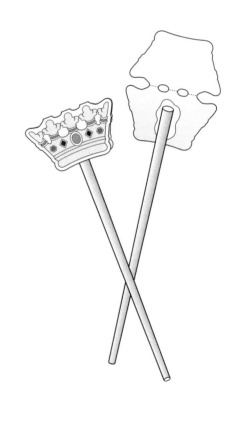

RCE28: Stand-up Temple

Supplies: Copies of the temple and HomeLink for each child, card stock, scissors, yellow cellophane, tape, colored markers or crayons, gold and silver glitter glue

Preparation: Copy the temple onto card stock. Cut yellow cellophane into three-inch squares.

Directions: Let each child cut out a temple outline. Help the children cut open the door on the solid lines and fold it forward on the dotted lines. The children should tape a piece of cellophane behind the door so it is seen when the doors open. Show them how to fold the tabs back to make the temple stand. Let the children decorate their temples by coloring and using glitter glue. Cut out and tape the HomeLink behind the yellow cellophane so that it is visible through the temple doors.

HomeLink 1 Kings 5:1—9:9; 1 Chronicles 29:1-9; Hebrews 9; Matthew 27:51

King Solomon built a beautiful temple where people could worship God. Jesus opened the way to God so we don't have to go to a temple to worship Him. Pray with your parents to thank Jesus for opening the way to God for us.

Suggestion: Glue or tape the HomeLink to the back of the temple, behind the door, so when they open the doors, they'll see the HomeLink.

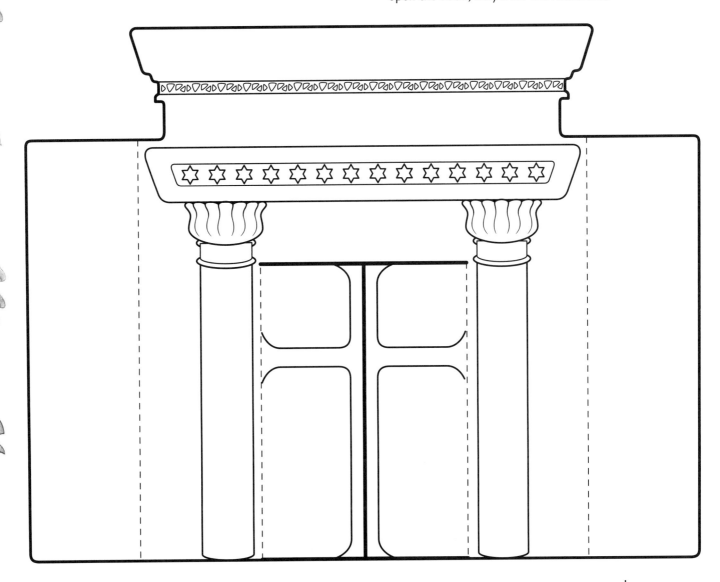

RCP28: Worship Doorknob Hanger

Supplies: Card stock or heavy paper, paint shirts, glue, washable water color paints, paintbrushes, salt in a shaker, small containers of water, copies of the HomeLink and doorknob hangers

Preparation: Make copies of the doorknob hanger on card stock, one for each child, and cut them out.

Directions: Have each child wear a paint shirt. First the children should glue a HomeLink to the back of each doorknob hanger. Then let the children paint the front of the hanger. While the paint is still wet, help each child sprinkle salt on the paint. When the paint dries, the salt crystals will glitter.

HomeLink: 1 Kings 5:1—9:9; 1 Chronicles 29:1-9; Hebrews 9; Matthew 27:51

Hang the doorknob hanger in a place where your child can remember to praise God. Review the Bible story with your child:

King Solomon built a wonderful temple. People could go there to praise God. The priests who worked there helped the people worship God. When Jesus died on the cross, people didn't need to go to the temple to praise God. We can praise God without going to the temple.

RCE29: Turn-around King Solomon

Supplies: Card stock, scissors, crayons or colored markers, copies of the HomeLink, (optional: gold glitter glue)

Preparation: Make a copy of the Turn-around King Solomon on card stock for each child.

Directions: Give out copies of King Solomon and let each child cut it out on the solid outline. Let the children color their pictures and glue a HomeLink to the plain inside. Show the children how to fold the figure on the dotted lines, folding both tabs back, to make it stand up. As an option, you could let the children use some glitter glue on the crown.

Let the children name choices to each other and use their Solomons to "turn their back" on a bad choice.

HomeLink
1 Kings 11–12

King Solomon knew the right thing to do, but he didn't do it. Tell the story of King Solomon to your parents. Talk together about things that might turn you from obeying God.

RCP29: King Solomon Stand-up Figures

Supplies: Set of stand-up figures and HomeLink for each child, crayons or colored pencils, scissors, tape, resealable plastic bags, (optional: fabric scraps, glue sticks)

Preparation: Make a copy of the stand-up figures and the HomeLink for each child. You may want to cut out the figures for younger children before class.

Directions: Give each child the four stand-up figures to color. As an option, you may let the children glue on fabric scraps as clothing. Show the children how to fold back the tabs on the dotted lines to make figures stand. Give children resealable bags with their names to keep the HomeLink and figures together.

HomeLink: 1 Kings 11—12

Today your child learned that Solomon let things turn him from God. Let your child use the figures as you tell the Bible story:

King Solomon made some bad choices. Set out the Solomon figure. **He did not worship God, so God punished him. Solomon's helper, Jeroboam, met a man from God.** Set out the Jeroboam and Ahijah figures. **The man ripped his new coat and gave Jeroboam 10 pieces of it. "You will rule over most of the people of Israel after King Solomon dies,"** the man said. **After King Solomon died, his son was a mean king.** Set out the Rehoboam figure. **Most of the people decided to have Jeroboam be their king instead.** Set out the Jeroboam figure.

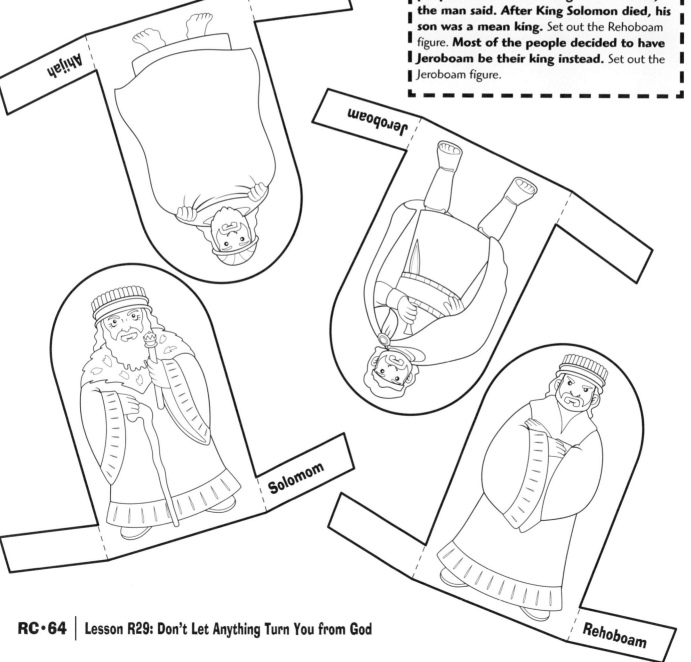

RCE30: Consequences Board Game

Supplies: Copies of the game board, crayons or markers, metal fasteners, paper clips, index cards, small squares of different-colored paper

Directions: Let each child color a game board. Hand out index cards, metal fasteners, and paper clips. Help the children draw one horizontal and one vertical line to divide an index card into four equal spaces. The kids should number each space, one through four. Attach the paper clip as the spinner by pushing the paper fastener through the card where the lines intersect. Have the kids follow the directions on each space of the game board. They each use a different color square of paper as a game marker. Allow time for the children to play the game with friends.

HomeLink: 1 Kings 16:29—17:6

Sin has bad consequences. Obeying has good consequences. Play this game with your family. Ask God for help in making good choices that bring good consequences.

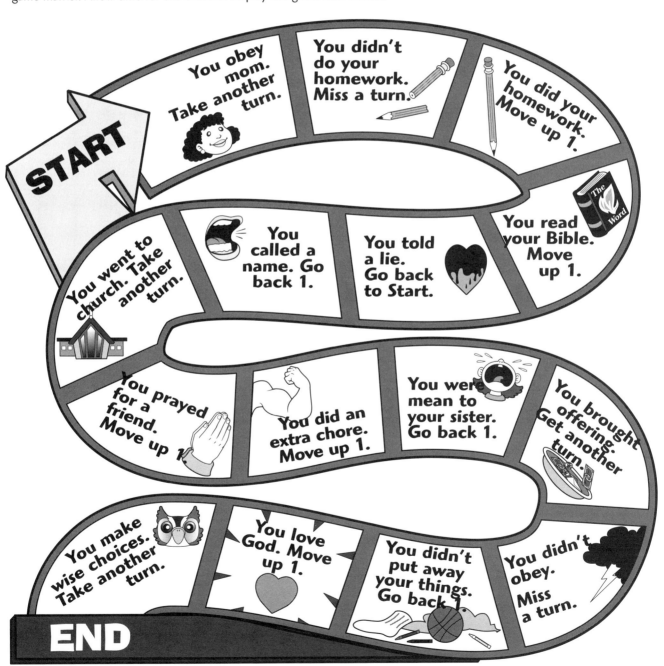

RCP30: Elijah Flannel Figures

Supplies: Copies of the flannel figures and HomeLink, crayons, scissors, glue sticks, 1" flannel squares, resealable plastic bags

Preparation: Make a copy of the four Bible story figures for each child and cut them out. Cut five one-inch flannel squares for each child.

Directions: Give each child a set of story figures to color. Show the children how to glue a square of flannel on the back of each figure. Help the children put their figures and a HomeLink in resealable plastic bags.

HomeLink: 1 Kings 16:29—17:6

In today's Bible story, Elijah told King Ahab that sin always has consequences. Use the figures to help your child review the Bible story. They will stick to textured fabrics, like a sofa.

King Ahab didn't pray to God. Have your child show King Ahab. **God sent Elijah to tell King Ahab what would happen because of his sins.** Have your child show Elijah. **Elijah said there wouldn't be any more rain for a long time. King Ahab was angry. God hid Elijah by a brook.** Have your child remove King Ahab and put up Elijah. **Elijah drank water from the brook. Birds brought Elijah meat and bread every morning and evening.** Have your child move the birds back and forth.

RCE31: "Trust God" Cube

School

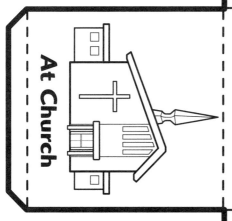

At Church

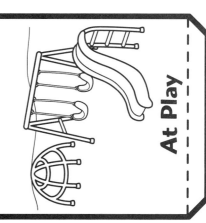

At Play

Home

Supplies: Copies of the cube pattern and HomeLink paragraph, crayons or markers, scissors, tape

Directions: Read the verse on the cube with the children. Let them draw a picture in each square showing a reason they would trust God for help. They should also think of their own situation to draw on the blank square.

Then let the children cut out the cube on the solid, dark lines. Show them how to fold on the dotted lines to form the cube. Tape the edges with the tabs inside.

The children can roll their cube and pray that God would help them in that situation. If they roll the Bible verse, have the children look up the verse in their Bible. Send a HomeLink home with each child.

HomeLink: 1 Kings 17:2-16

Elijah trusted God for the help he needed. God also helped a widow and her son. You can trust God for the help you need too. This week, each time you see a need, stop and pray about it.

Psalm 54:4 "God is my help."

RCP31: Elijah Hand Puppet

Supplies: Copies of the Elijah puppet pattern and HomeLink, lunch-size paper bags, scissors, crayons, glue sticks, (optional: fabric scraps)

Preparation: Make a copy of the puppet pattern for each child, and cut out the face and clothes. If you are using the optional fabric, cut pieces for clothes.

Directions: Have the children color their puppet pieces (or glue on fabric pieces) and show them how to glue the puppet pieces to the bag. The HomeLink should be glued to the back of the puppet. Children can make their puppets "talk" by moving the flap of the bag with their puppet.

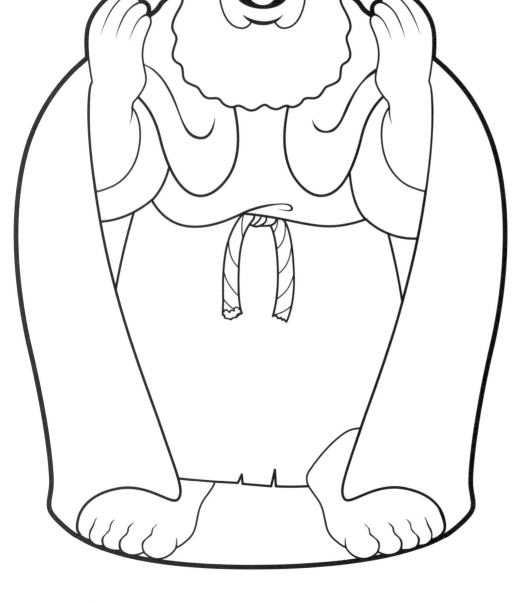

> **HomeLink:** 1 Kings 17:7-16
>
> God used Elijah the prophet to tell King Ahab there would be a drought. Elijah trusted God to help him when he needed food and water during the drought. Encourage your child to use the puppet during the week to act out the Bible story.
>
> **"I am Elijah. God told me to go to a town. A woman there would help give me water to drink and food to eat.**
>
> **"I met a woman by the town gate. She had only a little oil and flour to make a little bit of bread. But she made some for me and shared it with me. God kept oil and flour in her jars so we had food to eat every day."**

RCE32: My Mini Book of Prayers

Supplies: Copy of the three pages of the Mini Book for each child, scissors, pencils, stapler

Directions: Let the children carefully cut out the three pages of their Mini Book on the solid outlines. They stack them up, with the cover on the top right, and fold them *backwards* on the dotted line (so that the cover is on top). After creasing, the children should open their book to staple in the center, then fold again. Encourage the children to use the blank pages to write down things they pray about, leaving room to write how God answered.

HomeLink: 1 Kings 17:17-24

In today's Bible story you learned that God heard and answered Elijah's prayer. It is important to remember that God hears and answers your prayers. Keep a prayer journal to record answers to your prayers. Your faith in God will grow as you see all of His answers.

My Letter to God

Dear God,

_____

_____

_____

_____

_____

_____

Love,

My
Mini Book
of Prayers

The Amazing Answered Prayer

Not long ago, God heard a very important prayer. He listened carefully because He always hears our prayers. The prayer wasn't very big or very long. But it came from the heart. And God answered. He did not do exactly what was asked. But He did give the best answer. So remember, when you need to talk to God, He'll listen!

Winter, Spring, Summer, Fall, God hears our prayers and answers all!

Best Bible Verses Ever!

What are your favorite Bible verses? If you don't have any, ask your parents, teachers, and friends. Start making a list of verses that help you. See if you can find any verses about praying. Write them here.

_____

_____

_____

_____

HomeLink: 1 Kings 17:17-24

Home Sweet Home

Home wasn't so sweet for a widow and her son. The son became sick. He didn't get better. He died. The widow went to Elijah. She knew he served God. She asked him for help. Elijah went to the son. Elijah prayed. "O, Lord, let this boy's life return to him!" God heard Elijah's prayer and brought the boy back to life. God is great!

RCP32: Praying Hands Stained-Glass Picture

Supplies: Copies of the praying hands picture and HomeLink, colored pencils, cotton balls, vegetable oil, waxed paper

Preparation: Copy and cut out a picture for each child. Make a sample craft so you will know how it will work in class.

Directions: Set a piece of waxed paper in front of each child to use as a placemat. Lay a praying hands picture on top of each placemat. Let the children color their pictures with colored pencils. When done, children will use a cotton ball to dab a small amount of vegetable oil over the surface of the picture. This will give it a stained-glass look. Send the picture home on the waxed paper with a copy of the HomeLink.

HomeLink:
1 Kings 17:17-24

We can know that God listens when we pray, just as He listened to Elijah when Elijah prayed. You may want to display the stained-glass picture in a window. Share this version of the Bible story with your child throughout the week.

The woman's son got very sick. He got sicker and sicker. Then he stopped breathing. Elijah prayed. Then he lay down on the boy and prayed again, "Dear God, let this boy live." Elijah did this three times. Then the boy started breathing again.

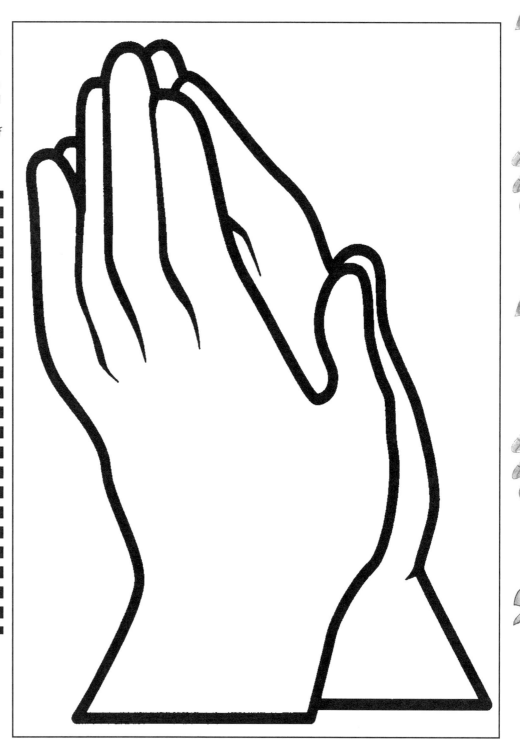

RCE33: Crown Windsock

Supplies: Copies of the windsock band and HomeLink, colored markers, scissors, card stock, glue, pencils, hole punch, stapler, crepe paper, (optional: gold glitter glue)

Preparation: Make a copy of the windsock band for each child. Cut card stock into 9" x 1" strips. Cut crepe paper streamers about a foot long.

Directions: Give each child a windsock band to color and cut out. Have the children glue their band to a strip of card stock, lining up the bottom edge. (The peaks on the crown will stick up above the card stock.) Have children write their names on the back. Help the children put the card stock in a loop and staple it.

Help the children punch holes in the three spots indicated. Show the children how to tie a short piece of yarn to each hole and then tie the three pieces together. They tie a fourth long piece of yarn where the three short pieces connect. This makes the hanger.

Let children glue or tape streamers to the inside of the windsock loop so they hang down. If you'd like, let the children add some light lines of gold glitter glue to their crowns to make them sparkle.

As the children work, remind them that there's only one God—He is the all-powerful King. Talk with the children about where they might hang their windsocks at home. Send a HomeLink home with each child.

HomeLink: 1 Kings 18:16–40

Elijah never forgot that there is only one God, even when 850 prophets of other gods stood up to him. Only God sent fire from heaven to burn up the altar.

God is more powerful than the wind, and He is king of the universe. Praise Him!

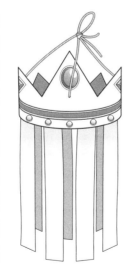

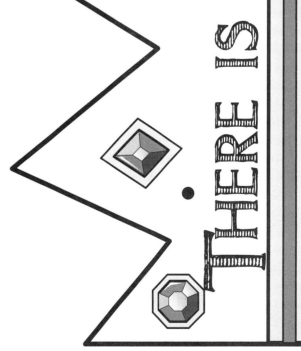

THERE IS ONLY ONE GOD.

RCP33: #1 Button

Supplies: Copies of the button pattern and HomeLink, crayons, scissors, tape, (optional: clear self-adhesive paper, card stock)

Preparations: Make a copy of the button pattern for each child. Use card stock for more durable buttons. If you have younger children, you may want to cut out the buttons for them ahead of time.

Directions: Let each child color a button and cut it out following the dotted line. As an option, you could cover each button (front and back) with clear self-adhesive paper so it will last longer. Use a loop of tape on the back of each button to fasten it on a child. Send home the button and a HomeLink with each child.

HomeLink:
1 Kings 18:16-40

In today's Bible story, the people of Israel learned that there is only one God. Your child made a button to remember that. You could tape a safety pin to the back of the button for your child to wear, or simply use a loop of tape to attach it to clothing.

You may use the following story to talk about the button with your child.

The prophets of the false god built an altar. They prayed and danced. But nothing happened. Elijah built an altar. He poured water on it one, two, three times. Elijah prayed. God sent fire from heaven. It burned up everything on Elijah's altar. There is only one God.

RCE34: Stone Reminder

Supplies: Copies of the "God cares" oval and HomeLink, crayons, scissors, one clean stone for each child (oval needs to fit on it), permanent marker, white craft glue in containers, paintbrushes, waxed paper

Preparations: Make a copy of the oval for each child. Wash and thoroughly dry the rocks.

Directions: Give each child a piece of waxed paper to use as a placemat. Let the children each color a "God cares" oval and cut it out. As the children color, let volunteers tell how God cared for Elijah in the Bible story. Also let children share ways God might care for them.

Have the children use a permanent marker to write their names on the bottom of their rocks. Help the children glue their oval to a rock. Then let the children "paint" a thin layer of glue onto the rock. Send a HomeLink home with each child's stone.

HomeLink:
1 Kings 19:1-18

Elijah was feeling awful, and God took care of him. When you're feeling bad, talk it over with your parents. Talk it over with God, too.

Put your rock where it will remind you that God is like a rock—He's solid and dependable.

RCP34: "God Cares" Heart

Supplies: Copies of the "God Cares" Heart and HomeLink, crayons, tissue paper, paper towels or bathroom tissue, tape

Preparation: Make a copy of the "God Cares" Heart for each child, and cut them out.

Directions: Give each child a "God Cares" Heart to color. As children are working, read the words on the heart. Talk about how God cared for Elijah when he felt bad. Help the children tape the edges of the heart together, leaving a small section open. Let the children lightly stuff the heart with tissue paper; then tape the opening shut. Pass out the HomeLinks to go home with the hearts.

God cares for me

HomeLink: 1 Kings 19:1-18

In today's Bible story, God cared for Elijah when he felt bad. Let your child use the heart pillow as a reminder when he or she feels bad.

King Ahab's wife, Jezebel, wanted to get rid of Elijah. He ran far away to hide. Along the way, an angel from God fed him. At a mountain where he rested, Elijah stood as God passed him by. First there was a big, strong wind, but God wasn't there. Have your child blow. **There was an earthquake, but God wasn't there.** Have your child stomp feet. **Then there was a fire, but God wasn't there.** Have your child rub hands together. **Then there was a whisper. It was God. God told Elijah he wasn't alone. And God would take care of him.**

RCE35: Gift Bookmark

Supplies: Copies of the bookmark and HomeLink, card stock or stiff paper, scissors, clear self-adhesive paper, yarn or gold embroidery thread, hole punch, colored markers

Preparation: Copy the bookmarks onto card stock or stiff paper and cut them out. Cut out rectangles of clear self-adhesive paper 6" x 8".

Directions: Give each child a bookmark to color. As the children color, talk about who they will give this bookmark to as a thank you for helping them learn about God.

Help the children peel off the backing of a piece of self-adhesive paper and place the bookmark about 1/2" from one edge. Fold the paper over the bookmark to cover the front and back. Then the children use scissors to trim the edges, leaving a little of the adhesive showing on all four sides. You may need to demonstrate this.

Help the children punch a hole in the top of their bookmarks and tie a length of yarn or embroidery thread through as a tassle.

RCP35: Bible Finger Puppets

Supplies: Copies of the finger puppets and HomeLink, colored pencils, clear tape, resealable plastic bags, scissors

Preparation: Make a copy of the four puppet figures for each child, and cut them out. Also cut out the neck hole of the cloak so it can fit over top of the Elijah and Elisha puppets without blocking their faces.

Directions: Give each child a set of four puppets, and let the children color the front and back of each. Help the children tape the edges of the Elijah and Elisha puppet to fit their fingers. Help them bend the tabs of the cloak and chariot puppets. The chariot puppet should stand up on the table. The cloak should fit over top of the Elijah or Elisha puppet. Put each child's puppets and a copy of the HomeLink in a resealable plastic bag to take home.

HomeLink: 1 Kings 19:1-18; 2 Kings 2:1-15

Today's Bible story of Elijah and Elisha shows how we learn from people who follow God. Have your child use the finger puppets as you read the following story.

Here is Elijah. Here is Elisha. Elisha is Elijah's helper. Elisha followed Elijah everywhere and learned all about God from him.

One day Elijah and Elisha walked along. They came to a river. Elijah took his coat and hit the water. It divided! Elijah and Elisha walked across on dry ground.

Elisha asked Elijah to pray for him. Elisha wanted to be as good a prophet as Elijah. Suddenly, a fiery chariot with horses came and separated the two men. Elijah went up to heaven in a whirlwind.

Then Elisha picked up the coat and hit the water. It divided! That meant that God had chosen Elisha to be His prophet and teach others about God.

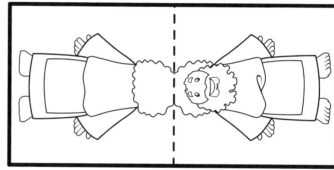

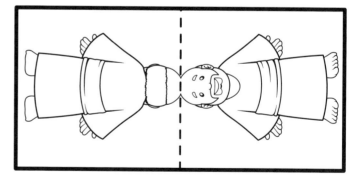

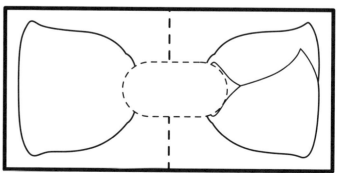

RCE36: Problem-solving Magnets

Supplies: Copies of the magnet and HomeLink, card stock, adhesive-backed magnetic tape, scissors, crayons or markers, stickers, (optional: cardboard)

Preparation: Make a copy of the magnet on card stock for each child. (Or copy it on regular paper and plan to let the children glue it to cardboard during class.) Cut the magnetic tape into strips about 2" long.

Directions: Let each child color the magnet and cut it out. Decorate the center with stickers. Show the children how to peel the adhesive off a magnet and stick the magnet to the back of the circle. Talk with the children about where they might put their magnets at home to remind them that God knows how to help them with any problem.

HomeLink: Daniel 2:1-49

King Nebuchadnezzar had a problem. No one on earth could help him. But God could, and Daniel knew it. Whenever you have a problem, talk to God about it. Pray with your parents about any problems you're facing right now. Put your magnet where it can remind you that God knows how to help you with any problem.

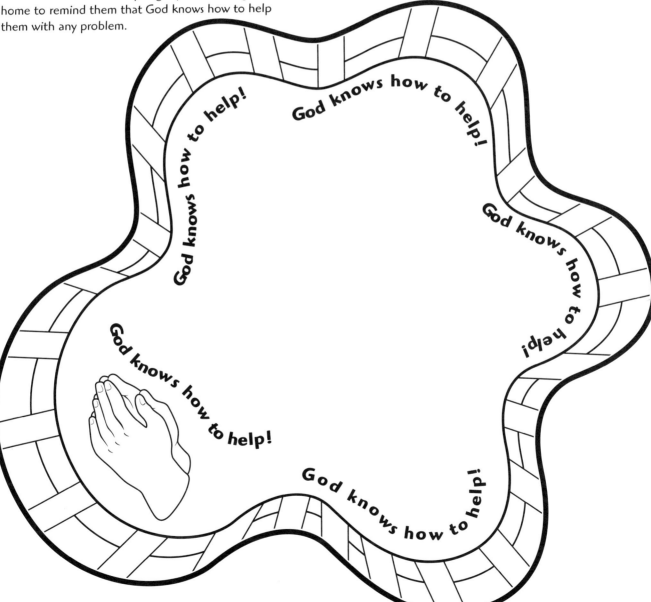

God knows how to help!

RCP36: Problem Box

Supplies: Copies of the pictures and HomeLink, small cardboard or plastic box or berry basket for each child, scissors, colored pencils, glue

Preparation: Copy the four pictures and a HomeLink for each child, and cut them apart.

Directions: Give each child the four pictures to color. Talk about how the pictures can remind the children that God knows how to help them with any problem. Help the children glue a picture to each side of their boxes. Glue the HomeLink to the bottom of the box.

At home, put in pictures of problems that you want to pray about in your box. When you pray, take out a picture and pray about it.

HomeLink: Daniel 2:1-49

Daniel prayed to God for the answer to a problem. Your child can learn to bring problems to God in prayer by using this Problem Box. After reviewing the Bible story with your child, talk about problems he or she might have. Work together to draw a picture of each problem. Put the pictures in the box. During prayer times this week, let your child pick out pictures of problems to pray about.

King Nebuchadnezzar had a bad dream. He wanted someone to tell him what the dream was and what it meant. Daniel prayed to God about this problem. God helped Daniel by telling him what the dream was and what it meant.

RCE37: Bible Story Diorama

Supplies: Copies of the Bible story figures and the HomeLink, crayons or colored markers, scissors, orange and yellow construction paper, glue, (optional: shoebox for each child)

Preparation: Make a copy of the Bible story figures for each child.

Directions: Give each child a set of four Bible story figures to color and cut out.

Give each child a piece of orange construction paper to fold into thirds. Have the children cut flames from yellow construction paper and glue them to the orange. They should glue a HomeLink to the back. The children may set up their orange "furnace" on a table and place their figures in front of it.

If you have a shoebox for each child, they may turn it into a furnace. Have the children turn the box over and trace the size of the box bottom onto orange construction paper. Let the kids cut flames from yellow paper and glue them onto the orange. Then they glue the orange paper inside their shoebox to make a furnace. They should glue a HomeLink to the back.

HomeLink: Daniel 3

Use your diorama to tell the Bible story to your family. Then talk together about how you can trust God to do what's right.

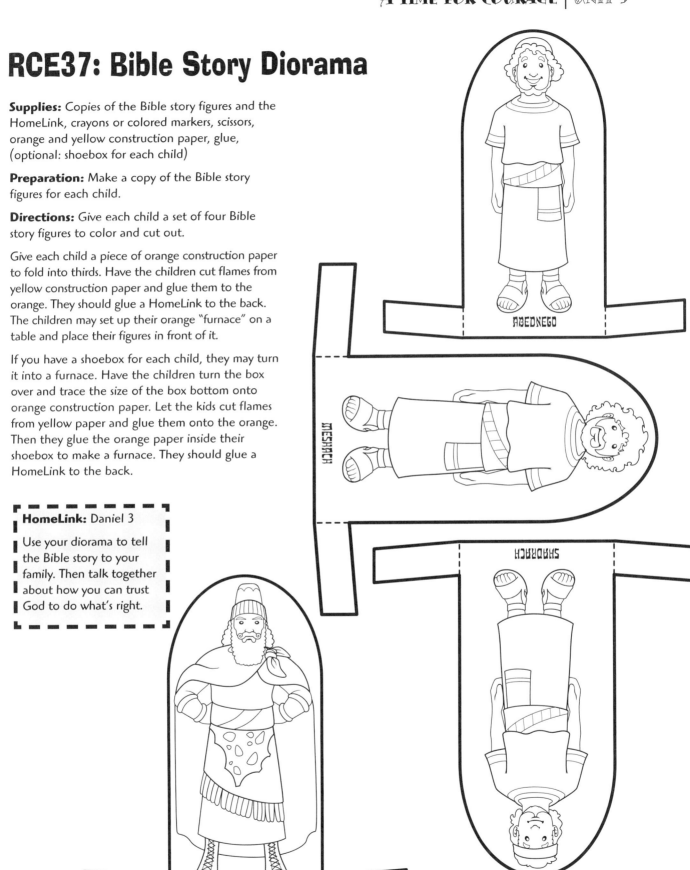

ABEDNEGO

MESHACH

SHADRACH

KING NEBUCHADNEZZAR

RCP37: Daniel Trading Cards

Supplies: Copies of the Trading Cards and HomeLink, scissors, crayons, resealable plastic bags, (optional: card stock)

Preparation: Copy the set of six trading cards for each child. You may want to use card stock for this craft to make the trading cards more durable. Cut apart the cards for younger children.

Directions: Talk with the children about who is on each trading card. Let each child color a set of cards. If needed, help the children cut them apart. Place the cards and HomeLink in a resealable plastic bag labeled with each child's name.

HomeLink: Daniel 3

Your child is learning to trust God and do what's right. Play this game to review the Bible story. Lay the cards face up. Read a sentence and let your child pick who it is.

I spy a king.

I spy a statue the king made.

I spy three men who didn't pray to the statue. They trusted God and did what was right.

I spy a very hot furnace where the king sent the three men.

I spy the angel in the hot furnace who kept the three men safe.

SHADRACH

FIERY FURNACE

GOLDEN STATUE

MESHACH

ABEDNEGO

KING NEBUCHADNEZZAR

RCE38: Break the Code

Supplies: Copies of code puzzle with the HomeLink, pencils

Preparation: Make a copy of the puzzle page for each child.

Directions: Give each child a copy of Break the Code to solve. Children may work together. Have Park Patrol workers help younger children. When kids finish solving the code, have them copy today's memory verse on the back using the same code key.

HomeLink: Daniel 5

Daniel showed King Belshazzar that God wanted him to worship and obey Him. The king brought disaster to his country because he didn't obey God. A nation that disobeys God is in trouble!

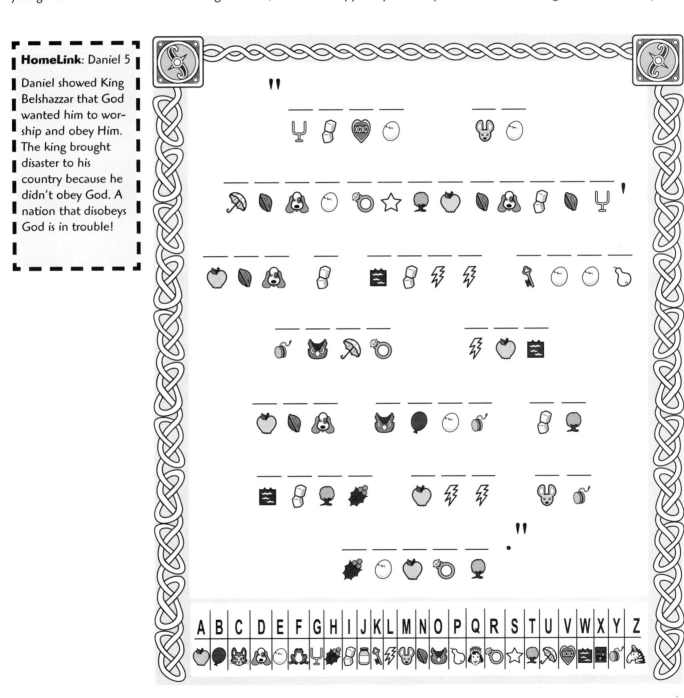

RCP38: Obey God Mobile

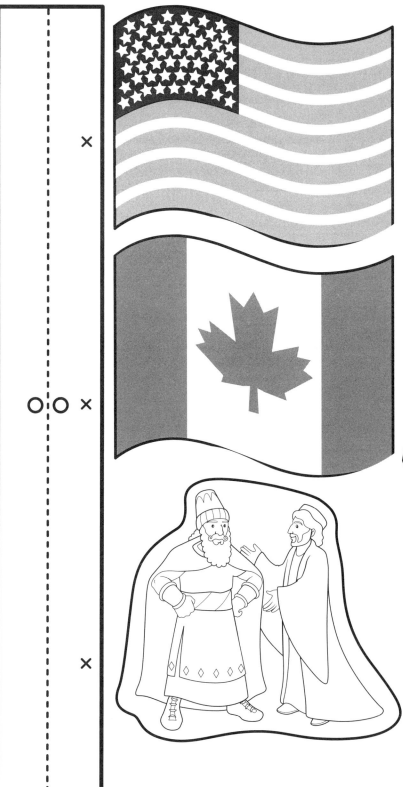

Supplies: Copy of mobile pieces for each child, crayons, scissors, yarn, tape, resealable plastic bags

Preparation: Make a copy of the mobile for each child. Cut out the mobile pieces before class if your students are too young to cut. Cut four six-inch long pieces of yarn for each child. Choose the flag for your country.

Directions: Let the children color the mobile pieces. As they color, talk about how the flag stands for your country. Show the children how to tape an end of yarn to each piece at the X. Then help the children tape the other yarn ends to the mobile strip at the X. Fold the strip on the dotted line and tape it shut. Tape one end of the fourth piece of yarn to the O on the strip as a hanger. Send the mobile and HomeLink home in a resealable bag labeled with the child's name.

HomeLink: Daniel 5

Today's Bible story showed how the king of Babylon lost his kingdom when he disobeyed God. Use the mobile to help your child remember to pray for your country and its leaders.

The king was having a party. He was using cups that belonged to God's temple. A hand appeared and wrote on the wall. Daniel told the king what the words meant. The king had disobeyed God. Because of that, the king was going to lose his kingdom.

RCE39: Heart Painting

Supplies: Sponges, marker, craft knife or scissors, duct tape, tempera paints in red and two other colors, paper plates, white craft paper, colored markers, salt or clear glitter

Preparation: Cut sponges in heart shapes of different sizes. (You may enlarge or reduce the pattern below and trace them onto the sponges.) You might make "handles" for the sponges with loops of duct tape about four inches long. Pour a little paint on each paper plate. Have enough for all the children to share.

Directions: Give each child a sheet of craft paper and let them write "Love God every day in every way" around all the sides to make a border. The children should add their names to the back.

Show the children how to dip a sponge in paint, holding the tape handle, wipe it on the edge of the plate, and then press it on their paper. One dipping will provide about two or three hearts.

Tell the children to leave their dipped heart sponges on the edge of the plate for others to use, and to use hearts that have already been dipped in a color—otherwise the colors will get mixed. Encourage the children to press a variety of heart colors and shapes on their papers, overlapping hearts and covering most of the surface.

When finished, set the papers aside to dry before sending home.

HomeLink: Daniel 6

Daniel loved God and showed it. We also can love God every day in every way. What are some ways you can show your love to God? Talk it over with your parents. Hang your heart picture where it will remind you to take time to show your love to God.

RCP39: Daniel Puzzle

Supplies: Copies of the puzzle and HomeLink, crayons, scissors, resealable plastic bags, (optional: card stock)

Preparation: Make a copy of the puzzle for each child. You may want to use card stock to make the puzzles more durable.

Directions: Let the children color the picture of Daniel praying. As they color, talk about what is happening in the picture. Help the children cut their puzzles on the dashed lines. Have the children put their puzzle pieces in a resealable plastic bag with the HomeLink labeled with their name.

HomeLink:
Daniel 6

Daniel prayed to God even though it meant he would be thrown in the lions' den. He showed that he loved God every day in every way. Help your child put the Bible story puzzle together. Then help your child retell the story with these questions.

Where is Daniel? What is he doing? If Daniel prays to God, he will be thrown in the lions' den. Find the lions. God kept Daniel safe. Daniel loved God.

RCE40: Changing Glitter Globes

Supplies: Baby-food jars with lids, permanent marker, water, baby oil, clear glitter, colorful sequins in happy shapes, craft glue, copies of the HomeLink

Preparation: Remove any labels from the jars or bottles. Use permanent marker to write children's names ahead of time, or let the Park Patrol help you do this during class.

Directions: When Paul met Jesus, Paul knew that he had changed inside! It wasn't that his face looked different, but now he was all stirred up about Jesus inside his heart and mind. We're going to make Changing Glitter Globes to remind us of the change that Jesus makes inside us when we believe in Him.

Give each child a jar. Let each child add two pinches of clear glitter and two pinches of sequins. Let the Park Patrol help you then fill each jar almost half full with baby oil. Children can participate by watching the pouring and telling the helpers when the jar is almost halfway full. Then fill the jar almost to the top with water. Leave a small space for an air bubble.

Help the children put a few spots of glue on the inside threads of their lids. Then they screw on the lids as tightly as they can. Double-check to be sure the lids are on correctly and tightly. Then let the children turn their globes over so they sit on their lids.

Show the children that when the globe sits still, the water and oil separate and the sequins fall to the bottom. But they can see the insides of the globe change when they swirl it around. Explain that when we get stirred up about Jesus, others can see a change in us and our behavior.

Give each child a HomeLink to set with their Changing Glitter Globe to take home later.

HomeLink: Acts 9:1-31

Paul had been out to get the followers of Jesus. He got them arrested. He hated them. Then Paul met Jesus on the road to Damascus. The bright light of Jesus blinded him, but more importantly, the meeting with Jesus touched his heart. Paul stopped hating and started loving. He knew Jesus was really who He said He was. Paul started telling everyone the good news about Jesus. Believing in Jesus changes us. Talk with your parents about what you believe about Jesus.

RCP40: Switch-Plate Cover

Supplies: Copies of the switch-plate cover and HomeLink, colored pencils or crayons, craft/utility knife, scissors

Preparation: Make a copy of the Switch-Plate Cover for each child. Carefully use the craft/utility knife to cut out the center rectangle for the switches. Cut out the cover outlines for younger children. Make a completed sample to show the class.

Directions: Show the children the completed sample of the Switch-Plate Cover, demonstrating on a room light how it fits over the switch.

Paul saw a bright light. He changed when he believed in Jesus. Let's make switch-plate covers to put in our rooms to remind us that Jesus loves us. Jesus appeared as a bright light to Paul. Whenever you turn on your light, this cover will remind you that believing in Jesus changes us.

Give each child a Switch-Plate Cover to color and cut out. Send home a HomeLink with each child.

> **HomeLink:** (Acts 9:1–31)
>
> Paul was changed when Jesus talked to him on the road to Damascus and he was blinded by a bright light. Use small loops of tape to put this switch-plate cover in your child's room. Whenever you use the switch, remind your child that Jesus loves each of us. Hearing about Jesus' love is an important part of your child's faithwalk.

RCE41: Willing Heart Sandals

Supplies: Craft foam in assorted colors, 1" craft foam hearts, scissors, 1/2"-wide ribbon, craft glue, ballpoint pens, copies of the HomeLink, (optional: hot glue gun)

Preparation: Cut sheets of craft foam into rectangles about 9" x 4" in a variety of colors, one per child. Buy or make 1" hearts from craft foam, assorted colors. Cut ribbon into 4-inch lengths, two per child.

Directions: Paul and Barnabas traveled all over, and many of their journeys had to be done by walking. In Bible times, people walked, rode donkeys, or sailed, and everyone wore some type of sandals. The sandals we will make today look like flip-flops, but they can remind us of how willing Paul and Barnabas were to travel all over and do what God wanted with a willing heart.

Have each child place one of his or her shoes on a rectangle of craft foam and trace around it using a pen. Get the Park Patrol to help the children do this. Then have the children cut out their shoe outlines. This forms the base of the sandal.

Give each child two ribbon pieces to place on their sandal in an upside-down "V," to resemble the straps on a flip-flop. The tip of the "V" should be about an inch or so down from the top of the sandal. The children may use craft glue to secure their ribbons to their sandals. You may find that a hot glue gun works best when gluing craft foam and ribbon. If so, operate the glue gun yourself, in a spot away from the children's craft table. The glue will dry in a matter of seconds so the children can move on to the next step.

Let each child glue a craft foam heart to the spot where the two ribbons meet. (Again, if using hot glue, do it for the children. Do not let the Park Patrol help with hot glue.)

Let the children use a pen to neatly print on their sandal: "Do what God wants with a willing heart." The children should also add their name to the back of their sandal. The children may use craft glue to attach a HomeLink to the back of their sandal, or simply send one home with each craft.

> **HomeLink:**
> Acts 13
>
> Paul and Barnabas did what God wanted with willing hearts. They traveled all over, walking, riding donkeys, and sailing. We may not have to travel far to do what God wants, but we can always have a willing heart! Talk with your parents about how you can have a willing heart to do what God wants.

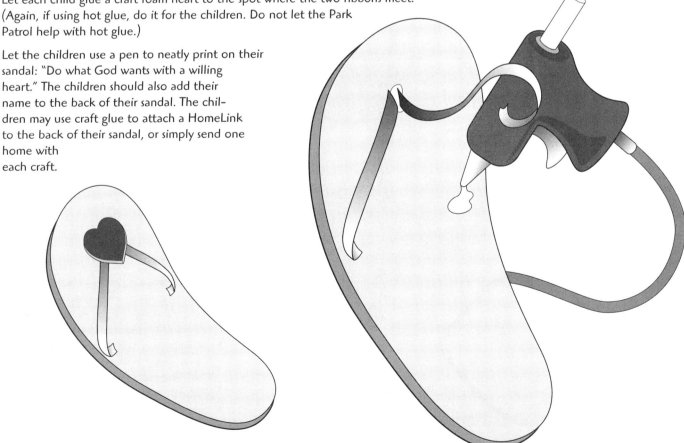

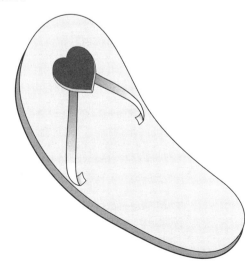

RCP41: Willing Heart Bracelet

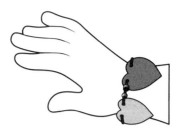

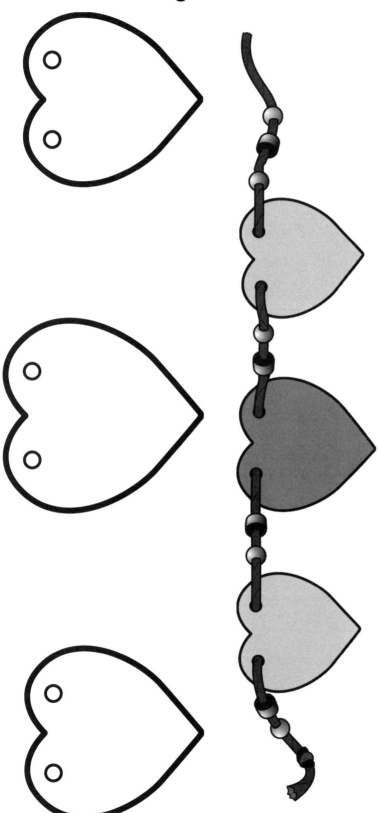

Supplies: Card stock or craft foam, hole punch or sharp scissors, 1/8-inch elastic cord, crayons, pony beads, copies of the HomeLink

Preparation: Copy the hearts below onto card stock or trace them on craft foam, making one set for each child. Cut out the hearts. Punch a small hole in each heart at the circle. Cut lengths of elastic eight inches long.

Directions: Give each child a set of hearts. If using card stock, let the children color them.

Give each child a length of elastic. Help the children thread it through the hearts, placing a pony bead between each heart. As the children work, remind them that Paul and Barnabas willingly did what God wanted them to do.

Tie the elastic to make a bracelet, making sure there is enough room to slide it over the hand. Send a HomeLink home with each child.

HomeLink: Acts 13

In today's Bible story, Paul and Barnabas did what God wanted with a willing heart. This is a hard concept for preschoolers. Encourage your child when you see actions being led with a willing heart. Let your child wear the bracelet as a reminder of Paul and Barnabas's good attitudes.

You may act out the Bible story with your child during the week. You might use scarves and robes for Bible-time clothes: **God told Paul and Barnabas to tell others about Jesus. They walked to cities. They rode on a ship. They walked some more. Everywhere they went they told people about Jesus.**

RCE42: Gift-giving Pouch

Supplies: Copies of the pouch and HomeLink, brightly colored or foil gift wrap, scissors, glue sticks, markers, (optional: card stock)

Preparation: Make a copy of the pouch for each child. As an option, trace the wallet pattern onto gift wrapping paper instead. Use the circle pattern to copy and cut out several coins for each child. Use gift wrap or card stock for the coins.

Directions: Give each child a copy of the pouch pattern, either on plain paper or gift wrap. Have the children cut on the heavy outline. Show them how to fold on the dotted lines. Help them glue the three flaps without writing. They should fold it so the writing ends up on the inside and they can decorate the outside with markers (or see the gift wrap on the outside).

Give each child a few paper coins. **What are some things that you can give because you love God?** (Part of my allowance, my talent of singing to God in a church children's choir, a helpful attitude with chores, etc.) Have each child choose "gifts" specific to them to write on their coins. Children keep their coins in their pouch . Give each child a HomeLink to put in their pouch.

HomeLink: Acts 19:21; Romans 15:25–27; 2 Corinthians 8:1–5

In our Bible story, many poor Christians gave money to help other poor Christians. They gave because they loved God. You can show your love for God by giving too. What can you give? Talk about some ideas with your parents.

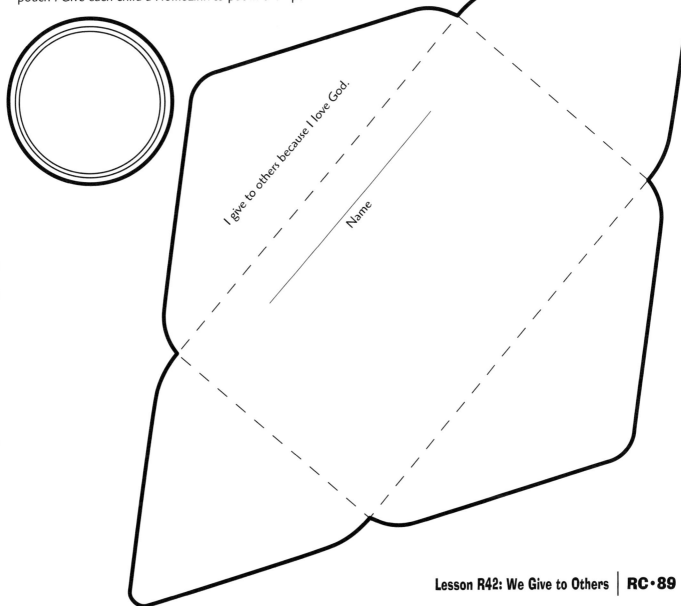

I give to others because I love God.

Name

RCP42: Offering Basket

Supplies: Copies of the picture and HomeLink, business-size envelopes (one per child), scissors, crayons, glue sticks

Preparation: Make copies of the picture and HomeLink and cut them out. Cut a handle in the flap of each envelope as shown in the drawing below.

Directions: Give each child a picture. Read the words together. Let the children color the picture of the people bringing money to Paul for the poor Christians in Jerusalem. Show the children how to glue the picture on one side of the envelope and the HomeLink on the other side.

HomeLink: Acts 19:21; Romans 15:25–27; 2 Corinthians 8:1–5

The churches in Macedonia and Corinth gave money to the church in Jerusalem during a time when the Jerusalem Christians were very poor. But they didn't give so that they could get paid back some day—they gave because of their love for God.

Let your child use the offering basket throughout the week as a way of reinforcing the concept. You may want to cut out some cardboard coins for your child to use. If you have a special project that your family is interested in, let your child learn how to give cheerfully to others.

Review the story with your child: **The people in Jerusalem needed money. Some people in another country loved Jesus. Their love helped them give money to the people in Jerusalem.**

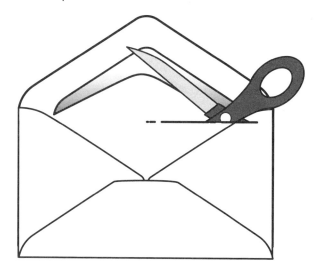

RCE43: Fingerprint Power Pictures

Supplies: White paper, washable ink pads in various colors, colored markers, wet wipes, glue sticks, copies of HomeLink

Directions: Talk with the children about things that Jesus has power over, especially things that the children might want reassurance about, such as storms, bugs, and so on. Also remind the children how Jesus showed His power through Paul in the Bible story, by healing the sick and bringing a dead man back to life.

Give out paper, and set the washable ink pads where all can share them. Show the children how to press a thumb or finger on the pad and then onto the paper to make a fingerprint. The children then use markers to outline the picture or fill in details. Show the children the examples on this page, or demonstrate for the children. Children will need to wash their fingers before using a diferent color ink.

Encourage the children to make pictures of things that Jesus has power over and to make several fingerprint pictures. They may want to make an "alive" person to show His power over death and illness. They may also make pictures of things they face that Jesus has power over. Children can explore with different sizes of prints their fingers and thumb make.

Caution the children not to rest their arms on just-finished prints or they will smear on the paper and leave ink on their arms. Have children add their names to their papers.

When finished, set the pictures aside to dry for a few minutes. Let children use wet wipes to clean the washable ink off their hands. They may each glue a HomeLink to the bottom of their picture.

HomeLink:
Acts 19:11-20; 20:1-12

Jesus' power is for real! He proved it through Paul. The sick were healed and the dead were raised to life. Jesus has power to help you, too. Pray with your parents to praise Jesus for His power. Ask for His peace and help for things you face.

RCP43: Paul Finger Puppets

Supplies: Copies of the puppets and HomeLink, scissors, colored pencils, resealable plastic bags, (optional: card stock)

Preparation: Make a copy of the three puppets for each child. You may want to use card stock for sturdier puppets. Cut out all the puppets, including the finger holes.

Directions: Give each child a set of three puppets to color. As the children color their puppets, review the Bible story with the children by asking questions about each puppet. Have each child put their puppets and a HomeLink in a labeled, resealable plastic bag to take home.

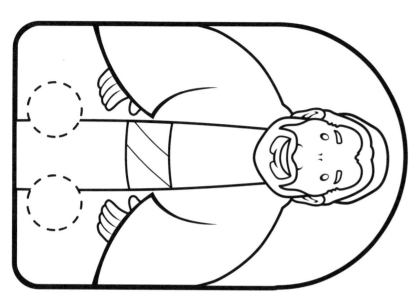

> **HomeLink:** Acts 19:11-20; 20:1-12
>
> Paul showed Jesus' power when he healed the sick and raised a young man to life. Let your child wear the finger puppets to act out the Bible story:
>
> **Paul traveled many places telling people about Jesus and His love. God worked many miracles through Paul. When sick people touched the cloths that Paul wore, the people became well. The young man Eutychus fell asleep listening to Paul. He was sitting on a window ledge on the third floor. When Eutychus fell asleep, he fell out of the window and died. Paul went to Eutychus and hugged him. Eutychus became alive!**

RCE44: Stormy Sea Crayon Rubbing

HomeLink:
Acts 21:27-36; 23:11-24; 27:1-44

In the Bible story, Paul went through very hard times! But he knew that God was with him and was helping him. God has promised to be with you in hard times too. Pray with your parents about hard times you are going through.

Supplies: Tagboard, plain white paper, crayons, sandpaper, corrugated cardboard, smooth cardboard, coarse fabric, glue, other textured papers, copies of the HomeLink

Preparation: Use these patterns to cut several wave patterns from textured papers, cardboard, or fabric (glued on smooth cardboard to make it stiff). Make a few ship patterns out of tagboard. Make a sample picture. Print "God is with me in hard times" on the boat.

Directions: Give each child a sheet of plain white paper. Set out the crayons, the ship and wave patterns, and your sample.

Paul was a prisoner on a ship when a hurricane struck! He went through hard times, but God was with him! A picture of Paul's ship will remind you that God will be with you, too, when you go through hard times.

Show the children how to place a wave pattern on the table with a sheet of plain paper over it. Rub a crayon lightly over the top to transfer the wave texture to the paper. Then choose a different wave pattern and rub another wave onto your picture.

Let children rub several wave patterns along the bottom of their paper to create the stormy ocean first. Last, they should trace a ship pattern on top of the waves.

At the top of their pictures, have children copy "God is with me in hard times." Then each child should glue a HomeLink to the back of their completed picture.

RCP44: Rock Paperweights

Supplies: Copies of the "God is with me" oval and Homelink, crayons, clean stones (that the oval can fit on), white craft glue in containers, cotton-tipped swabs, waxed paper, crayons (not markers), resealable plastic bags

Preparation: Make copies of the oval, and cut them out. Wash and thoroughly dry the rocks. Prepare one rock and one oval for each child.

Directions: Give each child a piece of waxed paper to use as a place-mat. Let the children each color a "God is with me" oval. Read the words together.

Help the children glue their oval to a rock, brushing the paper with a cotton swab dipped in glue. Then let the children "paint" a thin layer of glue over the top of the paper, overlapping onto the rock. When dry, send the stones and a HomeLink home in a resealable plastic bag. Write the children's names on the bags to identify them later.

HomeLink:
Acts 21:27-36; 23:11-24; 27:1-44

Paul went through many hard times when he was in jail and then shipwrecked. But God was with Paul in those hard times. The rock paperweight can help your child remember that God is with him or her in hard times.

Play the following game with your child. Use two chairs together for a ship: **Pretend to be Paul in jail. Now be Paul on the ship. What happens when the storm comes? Show me Paul getting to the beach. Who was with Paul?** (God.)

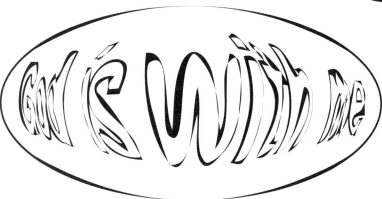

RCE45: Batik Promise Scroll

Supplies: Brown paper grocery bags, scissors, crayons (not markers or pencils), basin of water, paper towels, twine, copies of the HomeLink, (optional: dark watercolor paints and paintbrushes)

Preparations: Cut brown paper grocery bags into 6" x 12" rectangles, one for each child. Lay out newspaper to catch drips under the basin and to provide a place for the scrolls to dry.

Note: This craft is best begun earlier in the class time to allow for drying.

Directions: Give each child a brown paper rectangle to use as a scroll. Have the children use crayon to write in big, thick letters: God promised us a Savior. The children should further color all over both sides of the paper with crayon. Encourage them to make attractive designs or patterns. Children may find it easier to color with the long, flat side of a crayon.

One at a time, help children lightly crumple their crayon-colored scrolls, briefly submersing them in the bucket or pan of water. Help the children gently squeeze and shake the water out of their bags. Have the children spread out their scrolls flat on some newspaper to dry.

Before sending home, show the children how to roll up their scroll from both ends so the two rolls meet in the middle. Help the children tie a length of twine around their scroll to hold it together. Send a HomeLink home with each child's scroll.

Be sure the children know to unroll their scrolls at home to let them dry completely or the rolled scroll may mildew.

As an option, if you have time during class to let the scrolls dry, add this step before sending them home: Have the children brush dark watercolor paints over their scrolls, filling in all the cracks between the crayon marks. Keep paper towels handy for blotting excess. Once dried, the batik appearance is complete. The children may also do this step at home, or simply leave their scrolls with the "aged" look made earlier in class.

HomeLink:
Isaiah 7:14; 9:1–7; Micah 5:2

Many hundreds of years ago, God made a promise. He promised to send a Savior. He told the prophets Isaiah and Micah the details of this promise. Thank God today for keeping His promises and for sending the Savior.

To add to your Batik Promise Scroll at home, ask a parent to help you brush watercolor paints over the whole scroll, filling in the cracks between the crayon. Let the scroll dry completely before rolling.

RCP45: Prophet Puppet

HomeLink: Isaiah 7:14; 9:1-7; Micah 5:2

Prophets shared God's messages with His people. Encourage your child to use the puppet throughout the week to tell the promises of the Savior.

Isaiah was a prophet. He told about God's promise to send a Savior. He said that the Savior would be born to a young woman. He would come from King David's family. And He would have a special name that means "God is with us."

Micah was a prophet too. He also told about God's promise to send a Savior. The Savior would be born in Bethlehem.

Supplies: Copies of the Prophet Puppet pieces and HomeLink, lunch-size paper bags, crayons, glue, (optional: fabric scraps)

Preparation: Make copies of the Prophet Puppet pieces and cut out all the faces and clothes. Prepare one for each child. If you are using the optional fabric, cut pieces for the prophet's cloak.

Directions: Let the children color the puppet pieces. Show the children how to glue the puppet pieces to the bag. The HomeLink should be glued to the back of the puppet. Help the children make their puppets "talk" by moving the flap of the bag with their fingers.

In our Bible story, Isaiah and Micah told about God's promise of a Savior. Can you pretend that your puppet is telling about God's promise? Give the children time to make their puppets tell each other about the Bible story.

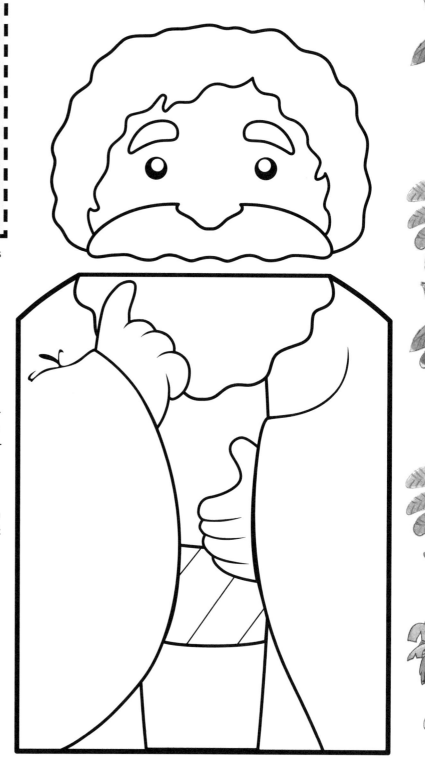

RCE46: God's Gift Pencil Topper

Supplies: Copies of the Pencil Topper and HomeLink, new pencil for each child, hole punch, scissors, colored markers or crayons

Preparation: Make a copy of the pencil topper for each child.

Directions: Give each child a God's Gift Pencil Topper to color. Be sure the children color both sides of it. Have the children cut out the present on the thick outline. Help the children carefully punch a hole at the top and bottom on the little circles. Demonstrate how to slide a pencil through the holes. When the children rub the pencil back and forth between their hands, the gift appears three-dimensional.

As the children work, discuss how this pencil topper can remind them of Jesus' being both God and human. **Jesus was born as a human baby, but He was God's Son. He was more than He appeared to be. This gift on your pencil looks like flat paper, but when you spin it between your hands, it appears to be 3-D.**

Be sure children add their names somewhere on their pencil topper. Give each child a HomeLink to send home with the pencil and topper.

HomeLink: Matthew 1:18-25; Luke 1:26-38; John 1:1

God sent an angel to Mary to tell her she would have a baby. But even better was that the baby would be God's own Son. God sent an angel to Joseph to give him the same news. Pray with your family to worship Jesus for being both God and human.

RCP46: Nativity Flannel Figures—Part 1

Supplies: Copies of flannel figures and Homelink, scissors, one-inch strips of felt (three per child), glue sticks, crayons or colored pencils, resealable plastic bags, (optional: squares of felt, thin ribbon)

Preparation: For each child make a copy of the Nativity Flannel Figures below. Cut out the figures for younger children.

As an option, you may want to create personal flannel boards for each child to use at home. For each flannel board you will need to make a small hole in the two top corners of a piece of felt. Thread one end of a 12-inch piece of ribbon through one hole and knot it so it can't pull through the hole. Repeat for the other corner.

Directions: Let the children color the figures of Mary, the angel, and Joseph. If not already done, help the children cut out the figures. Have the children glue a strip of felt to the back of each figure. Send home the figures and the HomeLink in a resealable plastic bag.

HomeLink: Matthew 1:18-25; Luke 1:26-38; John 1:1

For the next three weeks your child will be bringing home Nativity Flannel Figures. These figures can be used to review the Bible stories and to create a nativity scene for your child to use. The figures will stick to most fabric surfaces. You may want to put a piece of felt or fabric in a special place for your child to use. The following questions can help your child play and review the Bible story this week:

Who came to visit Mary? (An angel.) **What did the angel tell Mary?** (That she would have a baby, God's Son.) **Who else saw an angel?** (Joseph.) **What did the angel tell Joseph?** (Mary will have a baby, God's Son.)

RCE47: 3-D Shepherds Picture

Supplies: Copies of the shepherds picture and HomeLink, scissors, black or dark blue construction paper, craft glue, cardboard, pencils, yellow cellophane, cotton balls, white glitter paint or glitter glue, disposable bowls, cotton-tipped swabs, white crayons, colorful crayons

Preparation: Trace the outline of the lightburst onto cardboard and cut it out. Make a few so the children can easily share. Pour a little glitter paint or glitter glue into disposable bowls.

Directions: Give each child a picture of the shepherds to cut out along the outline. Each child glues this picture in the bottom left corner of a sheet of black or dark blue construction paper.

Near the upper right corner, have the children use pencil and a cardboard pattern to trace the lightburst onto their paper. Help the children cut out the lightburst from their black paper. Show the children how to glue a piece of yellow cellophane to the back of their paper to cover the lightburst shape and let the yellow shine through.

On the front, the children may glue small bits of cotton balls to the bottom of the page to represent sheep. They may use cotton-tipped swabs to "paint" glitter paint or glitter glue on the angel figure.

If children wish to add more detail to their 3-D pictures, they may draw with white crayon on the dark paper. They may also use colorful crayons to color their shepherds pictures. Be sure children add their names to the back and glue a HomeLink on.

HomeLink: Luke 2:1–20

Angels came to shepherds and said, "Good news! Jesus is born!" The shepherds went into Bethlehem to see baby Jesus. Then they told everyone the good news. Talk with your parents about why Jesus' birth is good news.

RCP47: Nativity Flannel Figures—Part 2

Supplies: Copies of flannel figures and HomeLink, scissors, one-inch strips of felt (three per child), crayons or colored pencils, glue sticks, resealable plastic bags

Preparation: For each child, make a copy of the Nativity Flannel Figures on this page. Cut out the figures for younger children.

Directions: Let the children color the figures of baby Jesus, the shepherds, and the sheep. If not already done, help the children cut out the figures. Have the children glue a strip of felt to the back of each figure. Send home the figures and the HomeLink in a resealable plastic bag, labeled with each child's name.

HomeLink: Luke 2:1-20

This is the second week in the series of Nativity Flannel Figures. Help your child use these figures to review the Bible stories. You may want to put a piece of felt in a special place for your child to place the figures on.

Mary and Joseph traveled to Bethlehem. They had to stay in a stable because the town was so crowded. Baby Jesus was born there. That same night an angel came to some shepherds. "Jesus, God's Son, is born!" the angel said. The shepherds found baby Jesus. They told everyone they saw, "Jesus is born!"

RCE48: Pocket Present

Supplies: Copies of the Pocket Present, scissors, glue sticks, tiny stickers (preferably Christmas), slips of colorful paper, pencils

Preparation: Make a copy of the Pocket Present for each child. Make an extra to demonstrate with to the class.

Directions: Give each child a copy of the Pocket Present to decorate with tiny stickers. Have the children cut out the large square and then cut only on the one solid line within the square. Instruct the children not to cut on the dotted lines. Show how to fold the panels back on the dotted lines so the words show. Children lightly use glue stick on the edges marked "glue here." On slips of paper, let children write down ways they can worship Jesus, such as *praise, love, pray, sing,* and so on. They keep their ideas inside the Pocket Present to remind them to give these presents to Jesus.

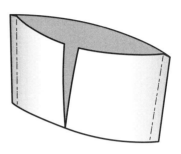

HomeLink: Matthew 2:1-12

The wise men gave gifts to Jesus, and they worshiped Him. What ways can you give the gift of worship to Jesus?

We give
the gift of
worship
to Jesus.

GLUE HERE

GLUE HERE

RCP48: Nativity Flannel Figures—Part 3

Supplies: Copies of flannel figures and HomeLink, scissors, one-inch strips of felt (four per child), glue sticks, crayons or colored pencils, resealable plastic bags

Preparation: Make a copy of the Nativity Flannel Figures below for each child. Cut out the figures for younger children.

Directions: Let the children color the figures of the toddler Jesus, the star, the wise men, and the camels. If not already done, help the children cut out the figures. Have the children glue a strip of felt to the back of each figure. Send home the figures and the HomeLink in resealable plastic bags, labeled with children's names.

HomeLink: Matthew 2:1-12

This is the last week in the series of Nativity Flannel Figures. Help your child use these figures to review the Bible stories. Since the wise men came at least several months after Jesus was born, your child may want to use the figure of Jesus as a toddler in this story.

Some wise men, who lived very far away, saw a star. They packed their camels and followed the star. The star led them to Jesus. The wise men worshiped Jesus as King!

RCE49: Eternally Turning Wind Spiral

Supplies: Copies of the HomeLink and rectangle below, toilet tissue tubes, colored markers or crayons, glue sticks, hole punch, scissors, yarn, (optional: shiny ribbon)

Preparation: Copy and cut out a rectangle for each child.

Directions: Give each child a copy of the rectangle to color. Help the children glue their rectangle around a toilet tissue tube so the lines match up. They will need to spread a thin layer of glue across the whole rectangle to cover the entire surface. Help the children punch a hole at the top where marked.

Have the children cut the tube on the thick black line to turn the tube into a spiral. When finished cutting, the children should gently tug the ends apart to separate the spirals. The children then tie a piece of yarn in the hole, allowing the spiral to spin freely.

As the children work, talk with them about where they might hang their wind spiral at home to watch it spin in the breeze. Discuss how it looks like it has no beginning and no end. Give each child a HomeLink to take home with their spiral.

If you have extra time, let the children tape lengths of shiny ribbons to the inside bottom of their tubes.

> **HomeLink:** John 3:1-21
>
> Nicodemus went to visit Jesus one night. Nicodemus knew Jesus taught the truth. Jesus told him, "You must be born again." Nicodemus didn't understand. Jesus told him, "You were born as a baby. That is the first time you were born. But you need to have God's Spirit in your heart. Believe in God's Son. That will be the born again part." Talk over with your parents what you know about Jesus. Hang up this Eternally Turning Wind Spiral to remind you that Jesus offers eternal life.

RCP49: Jesus and Nicodemus Puppets

Supplies: Copies of puppets and HomeLink, craft sticks, tape, crayons or colored pencils, resealable plastic bag

Preparation: Make copies of the puppets and cut them out.

Directions: Give each child a set of puppets to color. As the children color, talk about who the puppets are and what they did in the Bible story. When finished, help the children tape a craft stick to the back of each puppet. Place the puppets and a HomeLink in a resealable bag for each child. Label the bags with the children's names.

HomeLink: John 3:1-21

Jesus offers eternal life! He talked about this to Nicodemus one night. Let your child use the Jesus and Nicodemus puppets to act out the Bible story.

Nicodemus was an important leader. He came to talk to Jesus one night. Nicodemus knew that God was with Jesus by the things Jesus did. Jesus told Nicodemus that he needed to be born again. Jesus explained to Nicodemus that that meant that the Holy Spirit lived in a person's heart. That was when a person believed in Jesus. That person would go to heaven.

RCE50: Bookmark Reminder

Supplies: Felt and washable markers or vinyl and fabric paints or permanent markers; hole punch; scissors; cloth ribbon; copies of the HomeLink

Preparation: Use the pattern below to trace the outline of the bookmark onto felt or vinyl, making one for each child. Cut ribbon into eight-inch lengths.

Directions: Give each child a bookmark outline to cut out. Show the children how to cut the fringe on the bottom. Help as needed punching a hole at the top. For vinyl, you may need to poke the holes with sharp scissors. (Do this for the children.) Give each child an eight-inch length of ribbon to tie through the hole. Be sure the children put their names on the back.

On the board, print: "God sent His Son." Have the children copy this onto their bookmark. If using felt, the children may use washable markers. If using vinyl, the children may use permanent markers or shirt paints. If using paint, caution the children about rubbing their wrist in the wet letters they've just written. Set bookmarks aside to dry. Shirt paints will need 24 hours to completely dry; you may want to keep them until the next class, setting them in a place where they won't get bumped.

Give each child a HomeLink to take home with the bookmark.

HomeLink: Mark 11:27-33; 12:1-12; 15:24-39

God sent His Son to die for our sins. Jesus loves you so much that He wants you to live with Him forever. If you believe in Him and accept His sacrifice for you on the cross, you can join His family. Jesus loves you!

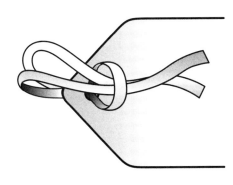

RCP50: Jesus Picture

Supplies: Copies of the Jesus Picture and HomeLink for each child, washable watercolor paints, brushes, water containers, salt in a shaker, paint shirts, scissors, gluesticks

Directions: Cut out the pictures and HomeLinks. After putting on paint shirts, let the children paint the pictures of Jesus. Have the children shake salt on the wet paint. When the paint dries, the salt can be brushed off. It will leave a pattern in the paint. Have each child glue a HomeLink to the back of a picture.

HomeLink: Matthew 3:13-17; Mark 11:27-33; John 5:36-37

In today's Bible story your child heard how God sent his Son, Jesus, to die for our sins. Help your child hang the picture in a special place for the week. You may want to use the following simple story to talk about the picture with your child.

John the Baptist baptized Jesus. The Spirit of God came down. A voice said "This is my Son." Jesus is God's Son.

Another day the leaders asked Jesus, "Who are You?"

Jesus said, "I am God's Son." God sent Him to die for our sins.

Jesus

RCE51: Gift Basket Service Project

Supplies: Basket (or box), items for a needy family, tissue paper, stamps and inkpads, stickers, ribbon, tape

Preparation: Plan to give a gift basket to a needy family in your church or community, or plan on a few smaller baskets that can be given to church shut-ins. If possible, send a note home with your students the week before this class asking them to donate specific items for the basket. Make arrangements to deliver the completed basket(s).

Directions: Tell the children about this service project: They will be decorating a basket to give to a needy family or individuals. You might briefly tell the children about the family or individuals. Set out the basket and the items, and let the kids tell why those items would be good in the basket. Then let the children fill the basket.

Spread out sheets of tissue paper on the table, and let the children decorate it by stamping decorative designs on it. They may also add stickers. When finished, help children set the basket on the paper, draw the loose ends toward the top and secure it with a ribbon. As an option, let the children wrap individual items in pieces of the decorated tissue paper.

Be sure to give each child a HomeLink to take home.

HomeLink: Mark 11:27-33; 12:1-12; 15:24-39

Jesus is God's very own Son. Because God loves us so much, He sent Jesus to die on the cross for our sins. This is an amazing gift to us! This week, you gave up your craft time to give a beautiful gift of your own to a needy person. You can keep on giving by praying for that person during the week.

This week, read the Bible story again with your parents. Talk about Jesus' death on the cross and thank God for His great love and forgiveness.

RCP51: Cross Craft

Supplies: Copies of HomeLink, craft sticks (two per child), red construction paper or craft foam, craft glue, washable markers

Preparation: Use the pattern to cut out a construction paper or craft foam heart for each child.

Directions: Give each child two craft sticks. Let the children decorate the craft sticks with markers. Show them how to glue the two sticks together to make a cross. Help each child glue a heart where the cross pieces intersect. As the children work, talk about how Jesus loves us so much that He died on a cross for our sins. Give each child a HomeLink to take home with the cross.

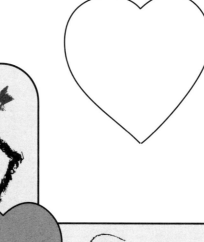

HomeLink:
Mark 11:27–33; 12:1–12; 15:24–39

God sent His Son to die for our sins. Jesus loves you so much that He wants you to live with Him forever. If you believe in Him and accept His sacrifice for you on the cross, you can join His family. Jesus loves you!

RCE52: Alive Again Picture

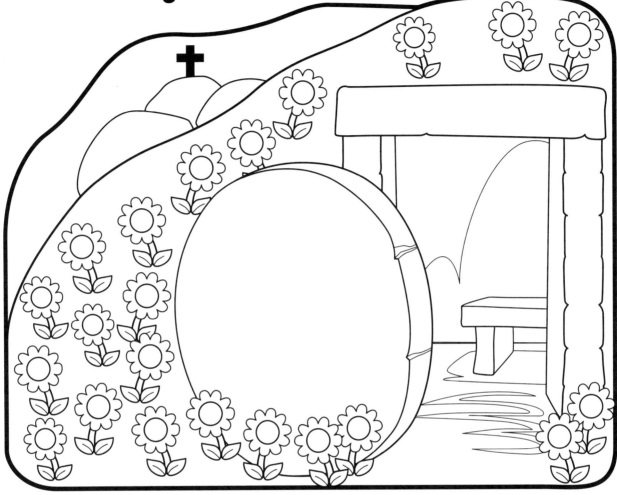

Supplies: Copies of the Alive Again Picture; scissors; yellow construction paper; one-inch squares of tissue paper in different colors; new, unsharpened pencils with flat erasers; liquid glue and glue sticks; small, disposable plates; (optional: crayons or markers)

Preparation: Make a copy of the Alive Again Picture for each child. Cut colorful tissue paper into one-inch squares. Pour a little glue onto each plate, making one plate for every two children.

Directions: Give each child an Alive Again Picture and have them cut it out on the heavy lines. They use glue sticks to glue it to a sheet of yellow construction paper.

Give each child an unsharpened pencil. Place a plate of glue between every two children to share. Children press a tissue paper square over the flat end of a pencil. (They may use either the eraser end or the flat writing end.) They use the pencil to lightly dip the flat side of the tissue paper into glue and then press it onto the picture on top of a flower. They repeat this until their picture is full of flowers. If time permits, let the children color the empty tomb and background.

HomeLink:
Luke 24:1-12;
John 10:17-18

Some women went to Jesus' tomb. Angels were there, but He was not! Jesus had come back to life! When the men went to check it out, it was true. Jesus is alive! Hang this picture where it will remind you that because Jesus is alive, He is always able to love you and be with you.

RCP52: Beaded Butterfly

Supplies: Copies of the butterfly pattern and HomeLink, chenille stems (two per child), 5–10 mm pony beads

Preparation: Copy the butterfly pattern and cut it out for each child. Bend each chenille stem one inch from the end.

Directions: Give each child a chenille stem and about 40 pony beads. Show the children how to thread the beads onto the stem. Have each child bead two stems. Bead all but three inches of stem on either end. Begin to form the butterfly by twisting the two stems together at one end by the first bead. (These unbeaded ends will be the antennae.) Then, count down 10 beads and twist the two stems together to form a loop. Repeat with the other stem, forming a second loop. Finally, twist each end again by the last bead where the stems were twisted before, forming two more loops. You will probably need to help the children twisting their butterflies.

As the children work, talk about how a butterfly reminds us of Jesus' being alive because a caterpillar looks like it has died when it spins its cocoon but it comes out alive—a beautiful butterfly!

> **HomeLink:** Luke 24:1-12; John 10:17-18
>
> Some women went to Jesus' tomb. Angels said that Jesus was alive again! A caterpillar spins a cocoon. When it comes out of its cocoon, it is a beautiful, live butterfly. The butterfly reminds us that Jesus will always be alive!

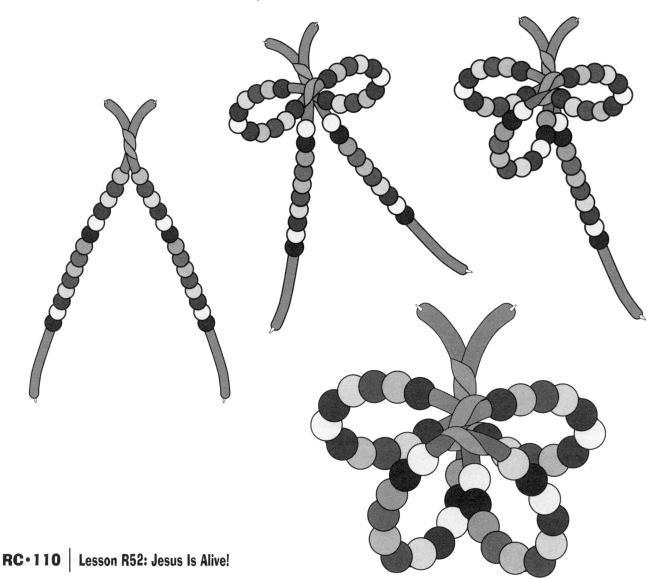

RCE53: Mini Bibles

Supplies: Shrinkable plastic, colored pencils, hole punch, crochet thread, (optional: scissors, access to an oven)

Preparation: Double-check that the brand and type of shrinkable plastic you chose works best with colored pencils; some need water-based pens or permanent markers. Determine if you may use your church's oven to shrink the finished plastic creations. If not, copy the baking instructions from the shrinkable plastic package and send home with each child. Think of a few short Bible verses that would be good for children to include in their Mini Bibles, such as shortened portions of John 3:16, 1 John 4:16a, or Psalm 119:105; print these on the board.

Directions: Today we've been learning that Jesus opens the Scriptures to us. He helps us understand what the Bible teaches. Let's make Mini Bibles to remind us of this. Give each child a half sheet of shrinkable plastic.

The Bible you draw will start out life-size. Before you draw, think of a plan in your head. You'll need to choose a color to make the outline of the open Bible. Then draw a line down the center to show the two pages on either side. Think of a Bible verse you can neatly print on your Bible. It could be our Bible memory verse, or another verse that I've written on the board.

You may want to draw the outline of a Bible and pages on the board to give the children an idea. Give the children time to draw and write. Some might choose to write their verse in colorful letters. Children may further decorate the edges of their Bibles with bright colors and patterns. When finished, punch a hole at least a half inch in from the edge in the center of each Bible. As an option, let the children round the edges with scissors.

If time permits, follow the instructions on the shrinkable plastic package to bake and shrink the Bibles to make Mini Bibles. If you can't shrink the Bibles during class, send home a copy of the baking instructions so parents can do this simple step at home.

To finish the Mini Bible, let the children tie a piece of crochet thread through the hole so they can hang it up or tie it to a backpack. Be sure to do this step *after* the craft has been baked and cooled.

For God so loved the world that he gave his one and only Son, that whoever believes in him shall not perish but have eternal life.

HomeLink: Luke 24:13-35

Jesus opens the Scriptures for us. He helps us understand what the Bible teaches. Hang your Mini Bible in a window or on your backpack. It will help you remember that the Bible gives us Truth for life.

RCP53: Bible Bookmark

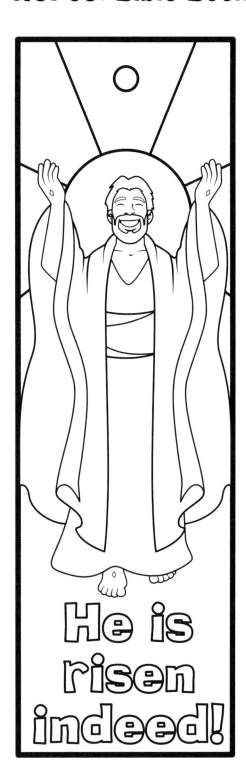

He is risen indeed!

Supplies: Copies of the bookmark pattern and the HomeLink, stiff paper (colorful, if possible), scissors, clear self-adhesive paper, washable markers

Preparation: Copy the bookmarks onto stiff paper, one for each child, and cut them out. Cut a piece of clear self-adhesive paper, 8" x 5", for each child.

Directions: Give each child a bookmark to color. Talk about the risen Jesus on the front while the children are coloring. Glue a HomeLink to the back of each bookmark. When finished coloring, fold the prepared clear self-adhesive paper in half. Take off the backing and set the bookmark on one half. Fold over the other half, sealing all the edges. Trim the edges to 1/2 inch.

HomeLink: Luke 24:13-35

The risen Jesus told all about God's Word to the men on the road to Emmaus. Use this bookmark in a Bible storybook for your child. Review the story together:

Two men were walking to a town named Emmaus. Pat your knees. **They thought they would never see Jesus again.** Make a sad face. **A man started walking with them.** Pat your knees. **He told them everything God's Word said about Jesus. The men stopped to eat. The man who had been talking blessed the food. Then the two men knew it was Jesus. Jesus left. The two men went back to tell others, "Jesus is alive!"** Pat your knees quickly.